T0300415

COST HALF : THE METHOD FOR RADICAL COST REDUCTION

COST HALF

....

The Method for
Radical Cost Reduction

TOSHIO SUZUE

PRODUCTIVITY
productivity press

Productivity Press • New York, NY

Most Productivity Press books are available at quantity discounts when purchased in bulk. For more information contact our Customer Service Department at (800)394-6868. Address all other inquires to:

Productivity Press
444 Park Avenue South, Suite 604
New York, NY 10016
United States of America
Telephone: 212-686-5900
Telefax: 212-686-5411
E-mail: info@productivityinc.com

Cover design by Steve Scates
Page composition by Carlisle Communications, Ltd.
Printed by Malloy Lithographing in the United States of America

Library of Congress Cataloging-in-Publication Data

Suzue, Toshio.
    Cost half: the method for radical cost reduction / Toshio Suzue.
        p. cm.
    Includes bibliographical references and index.
    ISBN 1-56327-249-0
    1. Cost control.   I. Title.

HD47.3 .S89 2002
658.15'52–dc21   2001058930

Contents

Preface

Cost Half is a set of cost reduction methods, a powerful program that achieves unprecedented levels of systematic organization. Pursuing the Cost Half approach is not a matter of making small, gradual improvements or piecemeal cost reductions, nor is it a temporary program of activities. After such programs are completed, things tend to revert to the way they were before. Instead, the Cost Half program creates a sleek but strong organization that embodies the idea of maintaining low costs while averting into backsliding after making progress.

A company executive once told me, "We've taken cost reduction as far as it will go. Our product can't be made any more cheaply." Despite the state of resignation apparent in these words, the man spoke proudly of his situation! Unfortunately, this type of attitude prevails at a great number of companies today. The following advice applies to all of them.

The "we've done all we can" attitude is premised upon the *current* product structures and production processes. It is analogous to a gardener who claims there's no better way to harvest fruit or prune his fruit tree—without changing the tree, that is. It's true—if you're not willing to change the current system, there is only so much that you can do to cut costs from it.

When you take the Cost Half approach, you soon run into this limitation, especially if you fail to precisely determine your goals for cost-cutting activities. It is not enough to set a goal of reducing costs by X percent. To establish effective cost-cutting activities, you must set goals that clearly address these two questions:

1. How are cost-cutting activities tied to business results?
2. What product-cost level is needed to ensure market competitiveness?

Once you establish goals that clearly address these questions, it becomes much easier to narrow your focus on cost-generating factors.

Cost Half Requires Developing Three Key Strengths

As we mentioned, the Cost Half approach does not rely on gradual improvement activities. Going back to the fruit tree analogy, a radical approach *does* go as far as replacing the tree, and this is exactly the capability of the Cost Half approach. It accomplishes this by developing three interrelated strengths that will also ensure stable business results.

1. *Market development strength.* Market development includes the ability to obtain customers and reach new customers. Having great merchandise and established distribution channels is ineffective if you lack market development strength. Conversely, market development strength must be premised on having good merchandise.
2. *Competitive strength in terms of quality.* In a nutshell, a "quality" product is one that doesn't break easily and that can meet users' needs. Naturally, the company that sells products and provides after-sales service is obliged to build such quality into its products.
3. *Competitive strength in terms of cost.* There are two key parts of cost competitiveness: one is the ability to ensure profitability, and the other is the ability to maintain appropriate product costs.

Any company that lacks all three of these key strengths naturally has a bleak future. Certainly, there is no chance that such a company could become a market leader. Of course, various efforts are needed to strengthen a company in these three ways. The question is, "Which strength should you target first?" Should the company select a theme that suits its particular environment? Should it combine that with a reshuffling of managers?

The fact is, these three strengths are so deeply interrelated that each one is like a different entrance to the same large cave—it doesn't matter which entrance you take to get inside. So the important questions are how to enter the cave and how to reach the point where you can appreciate how these strengths interrelate. On a basic level, they all support each other.

Low cost combined with poor quality will not gain a company new customers. Similarly, customers will not flock to a product that has good quality combined with a price that is above the market rate. In reality, the combination of high quality and low cost is mutually supportive. This is why it doesn't matter which strength you start with—if your efforts go deeply enough, with thorough, ongoing changes, the result is the same: a strong and stable organization. So the first question to ask when evaluating a cost-cutting program is not about which strength to implement first, but whether the program goes deeply enough and will be vigoroulsy implemented. In this book, our entrance to creating a strong company is *competitive strength in terms of cost* using the overall goal of the Cost Half objective.

The Cost Half Approach

The Cost Half approach is geared toward achieving two types of cost competitiveness: the *ability to improve the bottom line and the ability to maintain strongly competitive product costs*. Because of the need for quick responses to rapid changes in the market or business environment, the best approach is one that seeks to gain both of these abilities at the same time. Yet, shoring up profitability and holding down costs require distinctly different approaches. This is exactly what the Cost Half approach is designed to do. It uses a *two-way action* that pursues both of these objectives at the same time. Since approaches such as VA (Value Analysis), production improvement, and supply chain improvement do not attack the root causes of costs, they have only a limited scope of cost improvement and therefore are not aggressive enough for raising profitability and lowering product costs at the same time. This is where the Cost Half approach cuts straight to the heart of the matter—identifying and improving the places where costs are generated. This means, with the Cost Half approach there are no "sacred cow" cost generators in your company. As a result, there is no limit to the scope of improvements you can make.

Any company that fits one or more of the following descriptions is a prime candidate for establishing a Cost Half program.

1. A company that has tried various cost reduction methods but still needs a more thoroughgoing approach.
2. A company that wants to implement a cost reduction program that will yield clear results.
3. A company that recognizes cost competitiveness as its key strength and wants to further link it with human resources development.
4. A company that, more than anything else, needs to boost profitability and strengthen the competitiveness of its products.

Many companies already have been successful with Cost Half, and there is certainly much to be gained. [p. 4] And it would please me greatly to know that this book has helped at least one more company to revolutionize itself by boosting cost competitiveness first.

Acknowledgments

I would like to take this opportunity to express my gratitude to the people at the various companies I have worked with as a Cost Half consultant. My experiences in working with them have helped me to further refine this program.

In addition, I am also thankful to several of my colleagues in the consulting field for the experience and knowledge I have gained in working with them.

Finally, I wish to thank my publisher in Japan, Mr. Kazuya Uchiyama, for all of his hard work. My profound thanks also to Productivity Press, my publisher in the United States.

Toshio Suzue

1

Case Study of a Cost Half Project

Companies that achieve superior business results are those that continually implement various programs to lower costs, improve quality, and/or shorten lead time—all in an ongoing effort to improve competitiveness.

Various events trigger changes in markets and business environments, and each change can be seen as a useful opportunity to make a fresh analysis of the current situation. Companies that do not continuously adapt to the market will not survive.

EuZus, Inc.—a fictitious name for the subject of our case study in this chapter—had enjoyed a long string of good business results when their core products started losing their cost competitiveness to rival companies that were marketing lower-cost products.

This did not happen overnight. EuZus Inc. had been noticing that lower-priced competing products were entering the market in certain product categories. In hindsight, it was clear they had ample warning that they were heading for trouble. Though they had duly noted this trend, they failed to come up with any effective measures in response to it. In fact, they just decided to continue with business as usual.

EuZus Inc. was no stranger to cost-cutting efforts. They had carried out several programs before, all using similar types of cost reduction methods. Though they never managed to achieve the goals they had set for themselves, they had remained competitive. Moreover, because they had simply repeated similar cost reduction methods in each previous effort, both managers and team members suspected that there would be no end to their cost reduction targets. So they were at a loss as to how to respond to their present predicament.

The managers at Euzus Inc. realized at last that their old cost-cutting methods were ineffective. After searching around for alternatives, they decided to try a Cost Half project. About eight months later, EuZus Inc. began turning out products boasting improved cost competitiveness, and everyone was very satisfied with their successful effort to strengthen cost competitiveness. How did they do it?

EUZUS BUILDS A COST STRUCTURE FOR MARKET COMPETITIVENESS

EuZus Inc. had a long history as a designer and manufacturer of large machinery, one that would also modify its standard specifications to suit the requirements of customers who ordered custom-designed machinery. About half of the company's business consisted of such designed-to-order machinery. However, the departments responsible for design and production of these machines were showing poor business results. Although orders had previously been good, order volume was gradually declining, and it was not simply a matter of shrinking markets. EuZus Inc. was losing customers because their products were losing cost competitiveness. Naturally, they responded by conducting value analysis studies and trying to boost production efficiency. However, the cost gap between EuZus Inc. and its competitors only continued to widen.

EuZus' managers made a comparison study by examining EuZus' sales data spanning three years with that of a competitor, Zeycon Inc. (another fictitious name for this case example) (see Figure 1-1). The comparison data from three years ago is in the lower left part of the figure; the current comparison data is in the upper part.

When evaluating current results it is imperative to take into account recent trend data. Determining how things have changed over time can give you a clearer idea of what has transpired. You study market changes because cost competitiveness is market-based (change in market volume is indicated by a dotted line in each trend graph).

The X (horizontal) axis of each graph represents the range of product specifications. Products with higher performance and more advanced functions are positioned to the right of other products. The Y (vertical) axis indicates the selling prices of products. Looking at

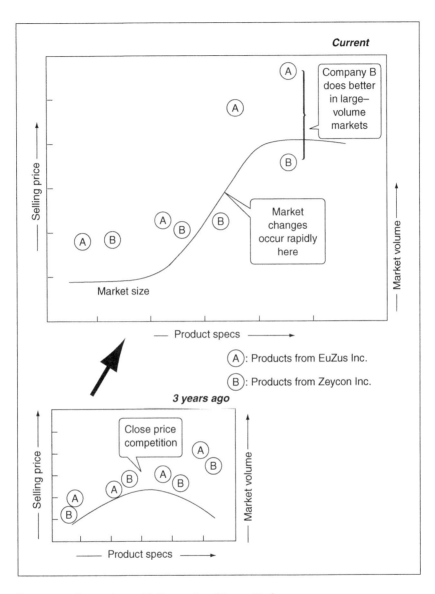

Figure 1-1. Comparison with Zeycon Inc. (Competitor)

these graphs, we can first note that the market's emphasis has clearly shifted to emphasizing high-end (higher performance, more advanced function) products—more so than it did three years ago. The general trend can be interpreted as a shift among ordinary consumers toward high-end products.

We can also see that, three years ago, EuZus Inc. and Zeycon Inc. were competing very closely in terms of product prices. Now, a large price gap existed between the two companies' products, especially in the high-end products, and this price gap developed during a time when the market size was expanding rapidly. Zeycon's prices did not increase much for high-end products. In other words, their cost structure did not change much according to the sophistication of its products. Zeycon had managed to create a cost structure that enabled it to set minimal price differences among its line-up of products.

While EuZus had clung to the market of the past, Zeycon had anticipated the future market by progressively targeting its fastest-growing segments. It was clear that Zeycon had refashioned its organization into one with lower cost levels. As for EuZus, the trend looked rather bleak, and employees at their factories began to think that, unless something changed, the company would find itself with no orders for its high-end products.

Pinpointing the Cost Levels

After making their comparison study, managers at EuZus Inc. grew acutely aware of the need to respond quickly to this situation, since a decline in their high-end product orders had already begun. But *how* should they respond? They certainly needed to develop new, lower-priced products; but not only that. After all, almost every Zeycon product was being sold for less than the competing product offered by EuZus. If EuZus were to introduce a new, low-priced product model, what would happen to its other product models?

EuZus *could* develop a whole new line-up of lower-priced products— but given their current development capabilities that would take about five years to accomplish. It so happens that—unlike Zeycon, whose development strengths lay chiefly in devising cost-cutting designs—EuZus' development strengths were in developing new kinds of products, and each new product took about 1.5 years to develop. Moreover, EuZus' managers did not have much confidence in their own cost-cutting abilities.

At this point they got in touch with a Cost Half consultant. They were aware of the Cost Half programs for creating a cost-cutting company organization and reasoned—correctly—that if they could transform their company into a lower-cost operation, they could assume that costs for the company's products would also decline. Soon they began checking their cost levels in order to determine a new set of cost-cutting goals and prepare for a Cost Half implementation. They studied trends among their sales results and major cost categories from the three previous years. Total sales (value-based) had increased slightly over those years, but their break-even prices had risen. As a result, they were facing a net loss for the current year. They noted various increases in their expenses over the years. The upswing was especially strong in indirect expenses. Figure 1-2 illustrates how many fixed-cost types of expenses grew.

The figure shows that sales expenses also increased during these years, meaning the company's efforts to implement lower-cost design for new products bore little fruit. One reason for this is that material costs and processing-related labor costs are the main costs that can be lowered by design changes, and both of these costs are variable rather than fixed.

Fixed costs, which do not vary in proportion to production volume, are more indicative of a company's qualities and strengths. These are costs associated with management and other indirect work. Fixed costs rise when there is an increase in the office equipment being used (information-processing equipment, for example).

The cost-cutting activities pursued by EuZus in the past were problem-solving efforts aimed primarily at reducing variable and

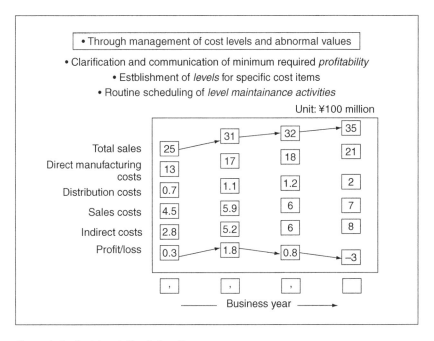

Figure 1-2. Cost Level Check Results

production costs that had risen slightly. A rise in production costs tends to create problems in terms of quality, delivery lead times, and distribution. Resolving these types of problems requires a variety of efforts centered on the manufacturing division, efforts that include boosting efficiency and eliminating sources of loss. But such efforts fall far short of the more radical cost-cutting efforts prescribed by Cost Half. Under this approach, EuZus was able to set target values for various cost items to help it pursue an initial goal of raising its profit level from the current $22,500 to $1,500,000 (slightly more than the company's all-time high profit).

At EuZus, a Cost Half project was organized during a preparation period of about six weeks, after which the actual Cost Half activities were launched. Although little time was needed to set targets and select participants for these activities, some effort was needed to persuade others in the company that this project was really necessary. The project organizers recognized that companywide implementation of activities was essential. They set a target value of 30 percent growth in sales volume (production volume), which was currently near an all-time low. This growth level corresponded to slightly less than the market share EuZus had enjoyed when it was competing head-to-head with Zeycon, and thus it was not an unreasonable goal. In fact, the survival of EuZus depended on competing strongly against Zeycon (and other competitors), so their goal of 30 percent sales volume growth should be viewed not only as reasonable but necessary.

Launching the Cost Half Project

EuZus' first step was to form four distinct Cost Half project teams.

1. Cost management team
2. Item cost reduction team
3. Process cost reduction team
4. Product cost reduction team

EuZus' goal was to reach a profit level of $1,500,00 and a reduction of product costs of 40 percent. To achieve this, the item cost reduction team and process cost reduction team were assigned the task of boosting profitability, while the product cost reduction team was put in charge of cutting product costs 40 percent.

The relationship among these teams is somewhat like the relationship between a railroad's trains and the tracks and stations that the trains use. Since there are many trains, it is impractical to try to cut operation costs on all of them. The better approach is to target a few trains for cost-cutting. However, cost-cutting activities directed at the train stations, tracks, and other hardware and software used by all of the trains is effective regardless of the number of trains. Thus, you should aim your cost-cutting efforts at both *item costs* (trains) and *process costs* (stations, tracks, etc.). Although total costs are the sum of these two cost categories, people tend to concentrate on item costs (individual products) rather than process costs. Forming effective cost reduction teams and setting target values are both very important steps in any Cost Half project.

As alluded to with reference to EuZus above, you can separate your costs into item costs (for physical objects) and process costs (for work processes). If each employee takes a good look around at the workplace, he or she will see various materials, parts, dies, spare parts, structures, storage rooms, and so on. All of these items are *cost generators*. The more there are of them, the higher your costs. You can further categorize these costs into material costs, parts costs, die costs, and so on. All of these fall under the general category of item costs.

By contrast, process costs are part of work and therefore are relatively invisible. Nevertheless, processes and people are needed to make the work happen. Process costs tend to increase as processes become more sophisticated and complex. This is reflected in specific process costs, such as personnel costs and office equipment costs. Figure 1-3 identifies most of these two types of processing costs. (To go into greater detail, we would need to set cost categories that suit a particular company's characteristics.)

The cost reduction teams at EuZus took charge of implementing activities to achieve the target profit level. Naturally, activities intended to make product pricing more competitive must focus on the next generation of products being offered to customers. These activities were assigned to the product cost reduction team. Meanwhile, the cost management team's mission included setting up and managing target values, as well as erecting and running a Cost Half management system. Their role included suggesting improvement themes that other teams could use in achieving their goals.

Training Team Members about Costs

A company should study its specific costs before deciding who will be on its cost reduction teams. Also, the different teams should be composed of employees involved in that area; for example, the product cost

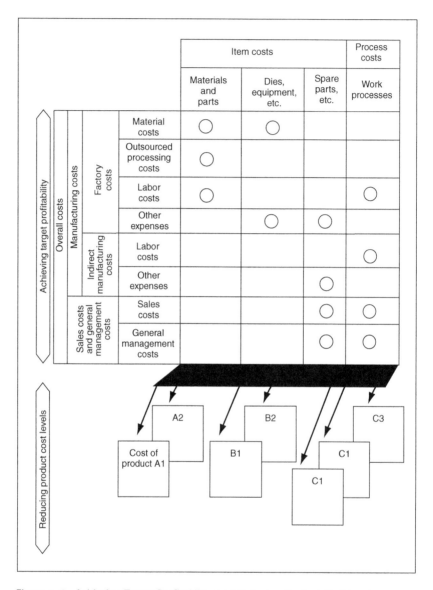

Figure 1-3. Achieving Target Profitability and Reducing Product Cost Levels

reduction team should include employees involved in the development of new products (new product models). Once you set up the teams, each team participates in two weeks (10 half-days) of Cost Half training. Such training is provided in parallel to the project's other activities.

During this training, we introduce the term *greedy eater* (see Chapter 2) to describe someone who is good at identifying cost generators and "eating" (eliminating) them to help reach the cost reduction target. Unfortunately, employees at EuZus were not very knowledgeable about costs. One cannot be a good cost cutter unless one understands costs!

Let's look at some misconceptions as to what constitutes cost-cutting.

Misconception 1: Costs are Basically Material + Labor Costs.   To be sure, the "materials + labor" formula is used when calculating costs for certain parts and the like. However, you must ask, "Exactly what kinds of costs are being included in the *material cost* category?" Does it consist of only the purchase cost of the parts at the time they are delivered? If we consider the parts supplier's perspective, the supplier incurred both *material costs* and *process costs* in making the parts. Once the parts are delivered to the purchaser, the purchaser considers their cost as entirely a "material cost." It is more appropriate to consider separately the cost of parts purchased from suppliers as *purchased goods costs*. In general, lumping these purchased goods costs together with material costs makes for simpler cost calculations, but then you are considering them only for a certain segment of time.

Studies intended to help reduce material costs often fail to clarify the points in time where certain costs become problematic. Furthermore, *cost reduction methods differ for material costs and purchased goods costs*. When target costs are not defined clearly, cost-cutting becomes difficult if not impossible.

People also tend to consider process costs in terms of "labor hours × wage rate." First, what is the wage rate? And how can it be reduced? When I asked those questions of employees at EuZus, they just looked at each other in bewilderment. They obviously hadn't dealt with such questions before. Predictably, none of them could think of any way to reduce process costs except by cutting labor hours. All other options were apparently "off limits" to them.

The way a person answers the simple question, "What are costs?" tends to reveal that individual's misconceptions about costs. Our discussion of this question helped EuZus cost cutters to better understand and analyze costs. To repeat: cost reduction activities are doomed from the start if the people involved do not really understand what costs are. For example, when I asked people the cost of the dies used to make sheet metal or plastic parts, invariably nearly all of them answered by referring to the purchase cost of the dies.

But what actions could you take to lower the purchase cost? You could simply ask for a discount in the invoiced purchase price of the dies, but that alone would not be enough. To fully understand the cost of the dies, you need to understand all of the costs that are incurred in the die-making processes. The first steps in die-making include drafting the part drawings and planning the production processes. It is essential you understand these planning-related costs, since various processes go into the planning of dies.

You must also understand the cost of drafting each die drawing for each die-making process, and find out the cost of making all of the dies' parts. Then there are the assembly costs, adjustment costs, and various other costs that are incurred after the die is made, such as the costs of mounting the dies in machines, test-operating them, performing maintenance on them, and so on. Only by totaling all of these costs can you determine the true cost of the dies.

In addition, since outside suppliers make most dies, the die costs include factors such as the supplier's own management costs and profitability level. Going over all of this together, EuZus' cost reduction team members learned what it takes to truly understand costs, as well as how essential that understanding was to effective cost reduction.

Misconception 2: Equivalent Parts Have Equivalent Costs. For most people, this is an article of faith. However, the fact is that the costs of equivalent parts often vary significantly. The reason is simple: *equivalent parts often have widely differing order specifications and purchase conditions.* And even when those factors are similar, costs (purchase prices) may vary depending on who is ordering the parts in question. Simply put, similar items can incur different costs.

At EuZus, I asked the cost-cutting teams to collect certain cost data from their own company. They were surprised to find different cost figures for parts that were equivalent in both name and function. This exercise underscored for them how examining costs can reveal areas that are ripe for cost-cutting. Figure 1-4 provides an overview of the training designed to make "greedy eaters" of the hitherto "clueless" members of the cost reduction team.

The figure's constellation of seven clues describes the knowledge and skills needed to succeed in the Cost Half approach. Each clue includes a set of techniques cost reduction team members need to learn, as well as ways to practice identifying certain parts or processes as cost-cutting targets. Once you have set up a group of cost-cutting targets, you can start devising Cost Half measures and estimating the capabilities that you will need to run and promote the Cost Half project. First, the cost reduction team members must get acquainted with the methodology, which has to go beyond a mere intellectual understanding; the cost cutters need to

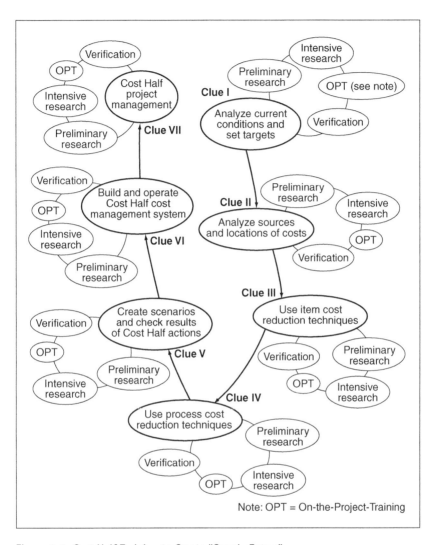

Figure 1.4. Cost Half Training to Create "Greedy Eaters"

learn how to recognize key points for cost reduction. To do that, they must practice using these methods until they master them, and must also pass certain tests to "graduate" from each of the seven clues.

At EuZus, 20 people managed certification in this training. Those people became the core group behind the Cost Half project and, naturally, the leaders of the activities performed as part of the project.

EUZUS INC. ACHIEVES ITS COST-REDUCTION GOALS

Six months after launching their Cost Half project activities, Euzus cost cutters had reduced corporatewide cost levels by 45 percent, which helped invite new product orders. Let's examine the makeup of this 45 percent cost level reduction.

By category, they achieved a 25 percent reduction in designed-to-order products, 46 percent in direct process costs, 57 percent in vendor's process costs, 44 percent in material costs, and 54 percent in direct costs. More specifically, they greatly reduced the number of parts, processes, and control points by improving the methods used for prototype testing and verification, fixed and variable structure designs, and designs to make products more compact and/or integrated. They also cut costs by using commercially available standard parts whenever necessary. Zeycon, which had enjoyed much greater price-competitiveness for its high-end products, had used similar techniques. When a new product order arrived, the product cost reduction team worked with the production line staff to execute the made-to-order product design. The resulting product was delivered seven months later.

As for the teams responsible for raising profitability to the $1,500,00 level, at the end of their activities they estimated that profits would slightly rise, exceeding their $1,500,00 target. They did this by focusing on distribution costs that occurred in administrative and design processes (and elsewhere). They innovated ways to reduce management costs and other indirect costs. As a result, they managed to raise the net profit to sales ratio to approximately 6 percent. Considering that this ratio had previously hovered around 2 percent, this was indeed quite an achievement.

What really amazed everyone at EuZus, though, was that they made these improvements during a time when the company's total sales sank from $26,250,000 to $22,500,00. No one doubted that the red ink would have been far worse were it not for these successful cost-cutting activities. A boost in sales began shortly after these activities were completed, but the lower selling prices meant that EuZus did not quite reach its sales target. Nevertheless, the company did manage to meet its goals in terms of market share and profit.

Subsequently, EuZus Inc. extended its Cost Half activities to other divisions and made it a companywide effort. After two years of Cost Half activities, they had integrated the methods used in the first Cost Half project into their product development processes and incorporated them into a Cost Half management system. This put them in the position to set new, even loftier targets for a second wave of Cost Half activities. One such target was to achieve a 10 percent net profit to sales ratio, and to do that they started new business operations and staff training programs. At this stage, their Cost Half activities had reached a new level of integrating their new business operations and staff training programs into a new Cost Half project.

From time to time in this book we will refer back to EuZus' success with the Cost Half project. Now we will move on to Chapter 2, which looks at some of the signs that indicate when it's time for a company to look into adopting a Cost Half program.

Telltale Signs that a Company Needs a Cost Half Program

If you have a roadmap, it's easier to anticipate what lies on the path ahead. However, very few companies actually adhere to—or even have!—a roadmap, since most of their managers tend to be buried in tasks related to day-to-day operations and solving current problems. Consequently, they miss valuable opportunities to adapt to the market and instead fall into a rut where the company's fortunes either stagnate or worsen.

When reviewing the reasons particular companies started a Cost Half project, I can tell which of them had a useful roadmap before beginning and which did not. The ones that didn't had a much harder time just getting underway, let alone implementing Cost Half activities. Employees in these "mapless" companies were less open-minded. Not only were they in trouble as regarded their market environment, their own business environment was also in poor shape. Also, they depended on more unnecessary labor-hours than did companies that followed a roadmap.

So, the important question is, how does a company develop a roadmap and stick to it? Determining this must come before all else. To maintain its competitiveness, a company needs to continually repeat the cycle of the following three actions.

Know ⇨ Find Out ⇨ Empower

FOUR SIGNS THAT INDICATE THE TIME IS RIGHT FOR COST HALF

Once you know that you have a problem, it's time to find out why. The following four signs are surefire indications that it is time for your company to consider the Cost Half approach.

1. Products lose their cost-competitiveness.
2. Cost structures become worse.
3. There is a marked increase in cost generators.
4. The cost management system lacks a repeatable management cycle.

We will take a quick look at each of these before we move on to Chapter 3, which focuses on empowering your company by implementing the Cost Half approach.

Sign One: Products Lose Their Cost-Competitiveness

Products lose competitiveness on the market when their appeal (marketability) to customers declines. Appealing products are those that strike a positive chord with target customers. When this appeal slips, it may be because the target customers have changed, the products are no longer able to strike a positive chord with them, or both.

In other words, this occurs when companies continue to pursue target markets and customers in the same old way despite the fact that target markets and customers are changing. When markets decline, sales of products in those markets also will decline. When that happens, companies must re-assess their marketing priorities.

In those cases where sales slump because a product has lost its appeal, the problem lies in the product's marketing concepts. However, in most cases, the real reason why products gradually lose their marketability, start losing out to rival products, and/or stop generating profits for the company, is that they have lost their cost competitiveness.

There is more to cost competitiveness than keeping costs at or below a certain level to help ensure higher profitability. Cost competitiveness also requires that the product in question be priced at a level that motivates people to buy and that it be presented as advantageous compared to rival products. Figure 2-1 illustrates an example of this from a Japanese company.

Figure 2-1 shows that, with each passing year, this company had fewer and fewer profitable product types, while their target markets remained the same throughout the period covered. Note that there

Figure 2-1. Find Out: ① When Products Lose their Cost Competitiveness

are numerous competing companies, so the products are always in competition with several rival brands. The competition is becoming so severe that you almost need to paste cash onto the products to sell them.

Finally, the company in question decided to move production to an overseas location with cheaper labor costs. This did not solve their problems, though, since their competitors had already done likewise and were running their own overseas manufacturing operations at lower cost. Clearly, the company's cost structure was too high and, unless such conditions were changed, the firm would continue to lose out to the competition. This is clearly a company that needs to discover the Cost Half approach ASAP.

Sign Two: Cost Structures Become Worse

As we saw in the case example of EuZus Inc. in Chapter 1, cost items that require investigation include those that have been clearly rising in cost trend data spanning several years. Some costs rise due to increased production output (linked, of course, to sales), but when such costs rise disproportionately, they must be studied. Consider for example material costs and outsourced processing costs. When the latter increase, this generally indicates a problem in expense outflow to contractors, suggesting that the company is not working hard enough to develop in-house capabilities. There's nothing wrong with having a well-defined outsourcing policy, and many companies with limited production capacity easily become dependent on outsourcing. But you still need to investigate rising cost trends. You also should check into product designs that call for greater numbers of parts, since such designs are another possible cause of rising material costs, outsourced processing costs, and purchased goods costs.

Rising costs may be the result of repeating a cycle of:

- higher sales
- more product models
- more parts
- more production processes
- higher costs

Management costs (including manufacturing management costs) and sales costs are basically fixed costs, so they are a separate problem. As their name implies, fixed costs are not related to production volume. Because the break-even point for products vacillates depending on production volume, even a slight drop in production volume can mean the difference between a money-earning product and a money-losing one.

Figure 2-2 illustrates a situation in which there are problems related to cost structure. As is shown in the figure, slight changes in production volume result in unnecessarily steep rises in fixed costs. Clearly, this is a sign that it's time for this company to pursue the Cost Half approach.

Sign Three: A Marked Increase in Cost Generators

Included in this category may be many items that you can sense and that are surprisingly important as cost generators; when, for example, you sense that certain phenomena have changed or that work is going less smoothly than usual. In short, you get a gut feeling that something is not right.

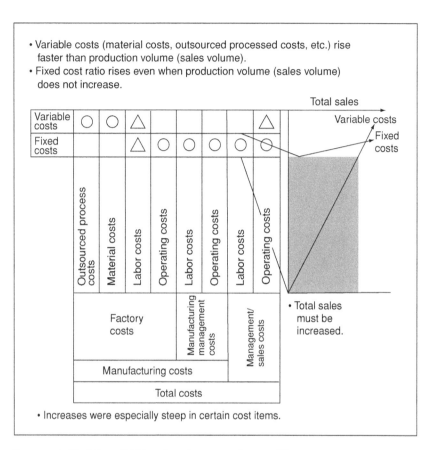

- Variable costs (material costs, outsourced processed costs, etc.) rise faster than production volume (sales volume).
- Fixed cost ratio rises even when production volume (sales volume) does not increase.

- Increases were especially steep in certain cost items.

Figure 2-2. Find Out: ② When Cost Structures Become Worse

Figure 2-3 lists many of the cost generators that we have typically encountered in Cost Half projects to date. The items listed here are problems that are generally sensed at some point during the product development or manufacturing stages. The costs generated by these items are due to unnecessarily large amounts of labor hours, parts, and/or processes. The figures for these costs are not directly visible and therefore generally require some review. Eventually, you will uncover these as factors corresponding to specific cost figures. In Chapters 4 through 6 you will find out more about the Cost Half approach and learn how these items correspond to cost figures. But a quick study of the Cost Half approach is essential in order to recognize the correspondences for at least half of these items.

• Cost generators
(Generators of work process costs)

No.	<Generators of work processes in R&D engineering>
	(Process costs from order reception to development, design, and manufacturing)
1.	Hierarchical, primarily team-based operations (organization/system)
2.	Inadequate source management of work tasks (passing work to the next process before completely confirming work quality)
3.	Inadequate concurrent management of work tasks (work tends to get delayed)
4.	Inadequate work flow management of work tasks (integration and linkage of R&D/Design with factory's indirect cost generators) (lack of professional management)
5.	Lack of coordination of reproducible processes from prototype to production stages (too many design revisions, too many trial runs)
6.	Poor communication during production setup and startup
7.	Inadequate tools (such as e-tools, CAD, CAE, CAM, and PMD)
8.	Inadequate development theme planning and improvement in reliability of specifications (many themes are too vague, development uses existing specs too often)
9.	Weak business development and client presentation skills (sales work that includes soliciting orders)
10.	Inadequate strengthening of design and engineering capabilities
11.	Failure to share expertise and data
12.	Failure to organize and design into fixed and variable categories (design methods are unorganized and vary among different products or parts)
13.	Lack of progress in organizational restructuring (share of purely technical work is 50% or less)
14.	Weak sense of teamwork and project-driven work (inadequate training and organization of professional managers)
	<Factory's indirect cost generators and work process cost generators>
	(Factory's indirect cost generators)
15.	Hierarchical organization
16.	Share of indirect task-related costs (converted to personnel costs) does not exceed 3% to 5% range
17.	Numerous control points
18.	Lack of progress in restructuring configuration of tasks (miscellaneous share exceeds 50%)
19.	Slow adoption of new tools for routine tasks (inadequate use of e-tools, etc.)
20.	Slow progress in restructuring of production management processes (too much inventory, too many delayed inventories)
21.	Slow progress in restructuring of quality control processes (too many defects and claims
22.	Slow progress in restructuring of work management processes for equipment, dies, jigs, tools, etc. (too many breakdowns, poor yield)

Figure 2-3. Find Out: ③ When There Is a Marked Increase in Cost Generators

	(Generators of product- and production process-related costs)
23.	Inadequate fixed/variable categorization of wide-variety production (too many production processes, piecemeal management)
24.	Inadequate fixed/variable categorization of specifications for products and parts (no shared items, piecemeal management)
25.	Inadequate fixed/variable categorization of product structures (no shared specifications, piecemeal management)
26.	Lack of progress toward multifunctionalization and consolidation of many parts and materials (too many parts and materials)
27.	Lack of progress toward multifunctionalization and consolidation of product structures (too many parts in product structures)
28.	Lack of progress toward multifunctionalization and consolidation of materials (too many materials in product structures)
29.	Lack of progress in optimization of raw materials, parts purchasing conditions, and purchase specifications (old habitual purchasing specifications are still used)
30.	Procurement is not from optimum sources or in optimum amounts (old habitual supplier selection and purchasing methods are still used)
	(Generators of production process-related costs)
31.	Inadequate adoption of process equipment for multi-function fixed and variable processing (too many equipment types)
32.	Lack of multi-function, consolidated processes, equipment, and dies (too many equipment units and dies)
33.	Lack of progress in improving processes by reducing labor requirements
34.	Lack of progress in improving engineering methods
35.	Too much quality loss
36.	Too much yield loss
37.	Too much loss due to equipment breakdowns
38.	Too much loss due to poor team management
	(Too many transport/distribution costs)
39.	Too many transport/distribution errors
40.	Loss due to rush shipments
41.	Loss due to damaged products
42.	Unsatisfactory lead times
43.	Poor work efficiency among work personnel
44.	Poor operating efficiency among equipment
45.	Poor vehicle efficiency
46.	Failure to review transportation structures
47.	Inefficient use of space
48.	Poor packaging efficiency

Figure 2-3. continued

Sign Four: A Cost Management System Lacks a Repeatable Management Cycle

Figure 2-4 shows how the cost management system can exist as a cycle.

First, you want to focus on the target customers to determine pricing that suits their needs. Then maintain a *design for cost* program to help realize the target pricing and implement improvement activities promptly in response to any abnormalities that occur. Track the results for analysis as trend data. Unless you repeat this cycle, the end result will be a loss of cost competitiveness on markets.

Naturally, companies have employees that are already in charge of cost management functions—but they are usually handling problems on an ad-hoc basis. That is, they are constantly busy devising responses to problems that are occurring, rather than attempting to devise preventive measures, such as implementing and repeating the cost management cycle in Figure 2-4. As a result, a company's cost structures may deteriorate—a clear sign that it is time to help your cost management employees by promoting the Cost Half approach.

So far, we have discussed four signs that indicate when it is time for your company to consider the Cost Half approach. Of course, the longer these problems persist, the harder it becomes to solve them.

And two more essential elements are required: desire and will

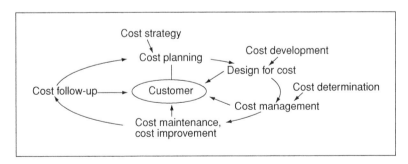

Figure 2-4. Find Out: ④ When the Cost Management System Lacks a Repeatable Management Cycle

DEVELOPING DESIRE AND WILL IN YOUR EMPLOYEES

Business is, in some respects, just a collection of numbers. On the other hand, the opportunity for implementing the Cost Half approach arises when managers have the desire and will to boost profitability, which means strengthening the infrastructure that supports the company's profitability. Business managers manage their various items by the numbers—i.e., as carefully obtained and controlled numerical values. But what can these managers do when the numbers start going downhill? The best solution is to find a way to make the company stronger so it can attain favorable results. This is where the Cost Half approach comes into play, because it builds an organization that generates lower costs while enabling the creation of a new product line-up. It also helps to inspire new work processes.

However, the objectives of the Cost Half approach include more than improving a company's worsening cost structure. It's also about implementing projects to build a stronger, more positive organization wherein all people have the will and desire to work together toward common goals. Since businesses are only as good as the people in them, human resource training is an essential part of the Cost Half approach. In fact, Cost Half activities function as a type of employee training experience, empowering employees via its methodology. So, though it may be true that business is just a collection of numbers, business mangers still must keep in mind the importance of human resource development in building the desire and will in the workforce to improve those numbers.

3

The Cost Half Program—A Way to Revolutionize Cost Competitiveness

Three characteristics—approach, actions, and techniques—distinguish the Cost Half program. Since the overall goal is to cut costs by half, you must have a general vision of what the company will be like as an organization generating only half of the costs that it does at present. After that, your mission is to make that vision a reality. In other words, when taking this approach a company sees that it is suffering high loss-related costs, and it acts to aggressively eliminate those losses. Although building up small improvements (reductions) in costs is important, it is not the same thing as the Cost Half approach, which is a "greedy approach" aimed at radically cutting costs by about half.

The actions performed via this approach are aimed at simultaneously achieving two goals: 1) competitive product pricing and, 2) profitability in target operations. Even when a company manages to lower the cost of a particular product, that is not enough to turn things around if the company cannot also manage to establish a stronger, more profitable business organization. Therefore, it is vital that the company implement a *two-way action* that works to achieve both lower product prices and a more profitable organization, as well as *five techniques* to change the cost-generating sources and locations.

To achieve this, the Cost Half program includes training courses covering those three characteristics—greedy approach, two-way actions, and five techniques—that form the basis of the Cost Half program. In this chapter we will explore a slightly expanded citation of these three key features. In Chapters 4 through 6, we will look more closely into the five techniques, since it takes a little practice to get the hang of using them.

A GREEDY APPROACH

The key word in Cost Half is *half*. Why half? Because when cost-cutting activities are based on a goal such as a mere 10 or 20 percent reduction in costs, people tend to come up with small, incremental cost-cutting ideas and are always conscious of the constraints involved. In other words, their whole approach is geared toward the modest goal of achieving a 10 or 20 percent cost reduction. You cannot revolutionize cost competitiveness by taking such a modest approach. So, the general goal is not modest but radical: *cut costs by half.*

When taking the Cost Half approach, people brainstorm using the mantra, "How can we cut costs by half?," to guide their repeated self-questioning as they seek to devise radical cost-cutting ideas. Some typical "cut-by-half"questions are:

- How can we cut the number of parts by half?
- How can we cut the number of production processes by half?
- How can we reduce a product's weight by half?
- How can we reduce the number of steps in this work process by half?
- How can we shrink development lead time by half?

And so on. In this way, the *concept* of "cutting by half " becomes the standard and measure of cost-cutting improvement ideas and provides a clear standard and a goal that can't be reached by devising small, incremental improvements. Instead, it promotes flexible, unrestrained brainstorming of ideas, because to revolutionize anything requires outstanding ideas.

Consider the life cycle of a company. At the outset, a company develops steadily, experiencing infancy, growth, and finally maturity. Eventually, it will enter a period of decline, but in the meantime the company's employees do whatever they can to extend its mature period for as long as possible. No one wants a company's life cycle to end quickly. As is shown in Figure 3-1, the market environment changes during any company's life cycle. Companies must therefore learn to reconfigure their operations in response to such changes.

During its infancy, a company must focus its energies on achieving specific product costs and improving quality, using techniques

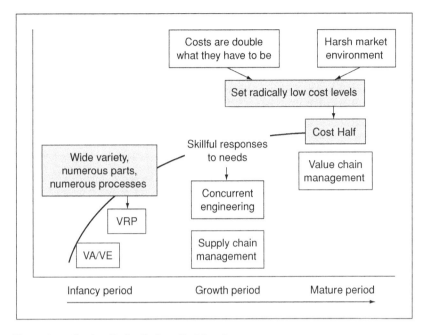

Figure 3-1. Setting Radically Low Cost Levels

such as value analysis. It is important that products are priced to sell and that their quality is high enough to avoid defects that can quickly make them unpopular.

As a company begins to produce and sell more products, customers become well acquainted with it. To meet the ever-expanding range of customer needs, it adds more variety to its product line-up. Many industries have entered an era of product diversification. Unfortunately, from the perspective of cost management, this translates into a greater assortment of parts and production processes—factors that make controlling costs more difficult.

When using variety reduction program (VRP) methods in response to customer demands, there is a need to pursue both greater, more efficient diversification and lower costs. To do this, VRP managers must divide their operations into those that positively contribute to diversification and those that require rationalization regardless of their variety. Meanwhile, they must also expand the company's operations in new, high-growth market sectors. At this point, the company has entered its mature period.

During this period, the company must build a product development system and a manufacturing/sales/delivery system, both of which are keenly attuned to new, emerging needs. Both concurrent engineering and supply chain management are useful in this regard.

Concurrent engineering revolutionizes the overall development process. It operates on three principles: 1) source management, 2) concurrent management, and, 3) flow management. (See the section in Chapter 4 entitled "Cost Half Technique 4.")

Supply chain management integrates all processes, from order reception to delivery, in order to provide products more effectively. However, despite efforts made in areas such as supply chain management, when a company's growth in production and sales begins to level off–i.e., when the company has entered its mature period–there is something else that must be taken into consideration: the investment figures for development, production, and business operations.

When a company's production and sales figures are on the rise, the amount of work naturally increases. To do the extra work, the company must invest in more staff, machinery, and other equipment. Problems can arise due to the fact that it is so easy to overinvest. After all, it is a relatively simple thing to hire more people and purchase more equipment in response to booming production and sales results. It is better, though, to first make improvements in work processes, products, and production processes before pouring in more investment money. It is also pays to make a special effort to ensure fully adequate planning. Still, in many cases, people feel forced by time constraints to devise response measures quickly, without thorough planning.

When a company overinvests, it does not take long before surplus staff and equipment are everywhere. Meanwhile, the market gets more and more competitive. And even in a growing market, you cannot expect too much from market growth if the number of competing firms is also increasing. In such situations, many companies belatedly discover that their employees, machinery, equipment, and so on have doubled. Hence, it becomes necessary to set an overall goal of cutting costs. This is where the Cost Half approach comes in.

Of course, the Cost Half approach does not insist on reducing *all* costs by *exactly* half. The point is that "half" should be used as the motivating concept when setting goals for cost-cutting activities. This "cut by half" ideal helps provide the backdrop for the greedy approach described earlier.

Figure 3-1 emphasizes the need for value chain management. When a company enters its mature period, it incurs unnecessary costs more easily but it still faces the imperative of having to create new value to survive. How will the company create new value? By developing and selling new products? By adding value to certain parts and units? By improving quality of service? Or by adding value in a roundabout way through other related products? The best way is to watch the market intensely while seeking to add new value; this is why many companies that implement a Cost Half project concurrently implement projects to launch new business operations, new products, or new services.

Implement Cost Analysis to Help Lower Costs

Figure 3-2 illustrates why companies need to switch from conventional cost-cutting activities to the greedy approach of Cost Half activities.

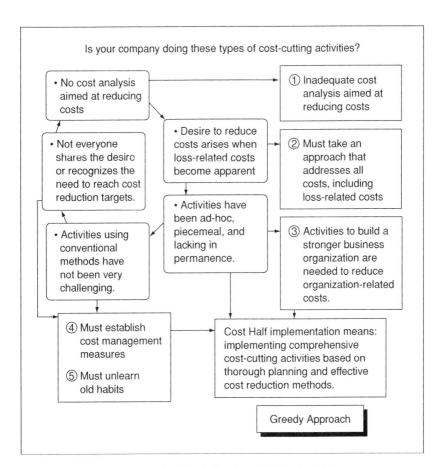

Figure 3-2. Things to Watch Out for during Cost-Cutting Activities

Obviously, you cannot reduce costs unless you first understand what the costs are, so cost analysis is an essential precursor to cost-cutting activities. This cost analysis is performed to get a general idea of where you are incurring costs, not specifically to lower those costs. For example, such an analysis would answer the question "What is the cost of this cover [a part]?" by presenting a pattern of information such as "The part's material cost is X and its process cost is Y." So, the cost information in the answer includes the various types of costs that comprise the part's total cost. We cannot say that such information reveals much about how to reduce the part's cost.

To undertake an analysis geared toward helping to reduce costs, you must collect specific information, such as determining which cost amounts and types (including material costs, process costs, etc.) are incurred and by which particular work processes or product parts. In a nutshell, your analysis must obtain specific information about specific costs. *The first element of the greedy approach does exactly that: it performs a cost analysis geared toward lowering costs.*

Figure 3-3 illustrates how the Cost Half approach divides costs into two categories: *things* and *processes*. In other words, you designate things and processes as separate cost generators. Things include materials, parts, equipment, dies, and other visible objects. Processes relate to the types of work a company performs and con-

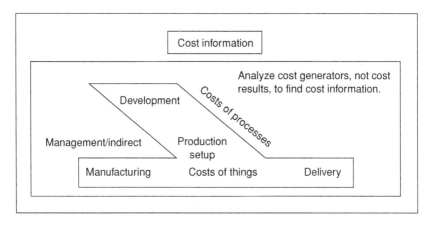

Figure 3-3. Analyze Cost Generators, Not Cost Results, to Find Cost Information

sist of many individual tasks. The more things there are in a company, and the more complicated the company's web of work processes becomes, and the more costs they incur. When a factory is chock-full of parts, materials, dies, and equipment, costs in that factory are obviously high. Likewise, when different divisions within a company duplicate work processes, or when significant backtracking or rework exist, it takes more people—or more time and trouble—to complete the work. In other words, costs are incurred according to how work processes are performed.

Consequently, analyzing quantities of things and process complexity is a step toward lowering costs. The analytical methods used in the Cost Half approach to achieve this are described in detail in Chapter 4.

Merely Eliminating Loss-Related Costs Does Not Radically Reduce Costs

If you walk through a typical office building or factory, you will come across nonstandard or even abnormal items and processes. Such nonstandard items and processes are manifestations of loss and include defective goods, malfunctioning equipment, line stoppages due to delayed supplies of materials, poor production yield, and idle time among equipment operators. Other examples include piles of in-process inventory, leftover materials, and used dies, jigs, or equipment. All are examples of waste, a form of loss.

To the extent that you can eliminate such waste-related loss, you can trim away these excess costs. However, even if you succeeded in getting rid of all waste-related loss, the resulting improvements would cut a factory's overall costs by no more than 5 percent. If waste-related losses of a factory are greater than 5 percent of total costs, then it is not a normal factory; that is, it is below average in terms of waste-related loss. When taking the Cost Half approach, be forewarned against the fallacy that eliminating waste-related loss is enough to radically reduce costs.

Thus, *the second element of the greedy approach is that it seeks to cut costs by creating a strong company organization.* The major goals of the Cost Half approach, then, are to achieve product pricing that is highly market-competitive and to ensure satisfactory profitability from the company's business operations.

Replace Previous Cost-Cutting Activities with Systematic Activities

Many companies perform cost-cutting activities out of habit or on an ad-hoc basis. The Cost Half approach replaces these tactics with well-organized, systematic activities. One typical pattern for conventional cost-cutting efforts is the habit of having the cost management division assign cost reduction targets to design departments, factories, and so on. They then leave it up to the respective staffs to come up with cost-cutting ideas to achieve these targets. Using the same old cost-cutting concepts and methods, the staffs plod away and somehow muddle through. If they fail to achieve their assigned targets, they launch a new round of stale activities, or they just give up. The characteristics of this type of conventional approach to cost-cutting are as follows.

- Cost-cutting activities are ad-hoc, transient activities that are not likely to amount to much.
- Activities do not go "outside the box" of customary scope and methods.
- Targets are vague and rarely inspire the people who are supposed to achieve them.

This conventional approach is unlikely to launch cost-cutting activities that strengthen and reinvigorate the company. Consequently, *the third element of the greedy approach is that it involves new types of cost-cutting activities that go beyond the old, conventional methods.* As such, the greedy approach works to improve the quality of Cost Half activities. In other words, it establishes Cost Half activities as an integral part of the company's system for making improvements and as part of its cost management system.

The greedy approach requires that many of the people involved learn Cost Half techniques, and that cost-generating sources and locations are first identified via a flexible analysis that is not hindered by the company's divisional or in-house/external barriers. It also requires the cultivation of leaders who can handle the operation of a Cost Half project and support activities that help meet these requirements.

TWO-WAY ACTION

We have already seen how cost generators can be divided according to item costs and process costs. Dividing cost generators in this way supports a logical approach for reducing fixed costs, which has always been a cost-cutting goal.

As Figure 3-4 shows, item costs include the expenses incurred for product materials and parts as well as equipment and dies that are used to process and assemble these materials and parts. Ordinarily, a normally functioning manufacturer will have developed a production and sales system that can handle a wide variety of products. Consequently, the company uses large quantities of parts, materials, equipment, and dies (referred to as items or things). To the extent that such items exist in a company, they are obviously cost generators. To the extent that excess amounts of such items exist, the company is burdened with excessive costs. The existence of these items is inseparable from the company's products—if there were no products, none of these items would exist, and there would be no item costs.

As we stated earlier, it is vital that the company implement a *two-way action* that works to achieve both lower product prices and a more profitable organization. The first way focuses on reducing item costs; the second way focuses on reducing process costs.

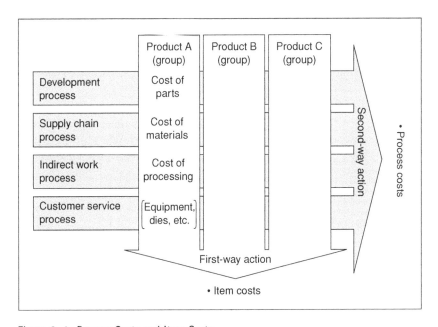

Figure 3-4. Process Costs and Item Costs

As regards the first way, your first step is to establish as targets for cost-cutting *all item costs* related to visible items, including costs incurred by materials, parts, equipment, and dies. Although this step can be implemented without any connection to product development, the fact is that suggestions generated with product design changes in mind are more effective and farther-reaching in scope than those generated with no consideration of product design. However, given the time required to produce such suggestions, and the timing-related issues involved in acting upon them, it is a good idea during the first step to limit the scope of cost-cutting activities to avoid design changes. As a second step, you can expand the scope to include design changes.

By contrast, *process costs* are expenses incurred when performing development, production management, and supply chain work processes. These costs are broken down according to the work process flows that occur for different types of work. Thus, process costs and item costs arise from different cost generators. Accordingly, Cost Half uses a different method—in this case, the second way of the two-way action—to handle process costs. During Cost Half implementation, it is both necessary and efficacious to apply different optimal methods for different types of cost-generating sources and locations.

The Cost Half approach means implementing the first way and second way of the two-way action simultaneously. But if you look at the bottom of Figure 3-5, you will see that the term "two-way action" also has another meaning.

The objective of Cost Half activities is to establish competitive product cost levels while ensuring the desired level of profitability. The first part of the two-way action establishes competitive product cost levels by focusing activities on the most important products being developed and marketed. Naturally, that includes activities focused on the parts or materials that go into these products.

The second part of the two-way action is to implement activities designed to ensure the target level of profitability. To do this, the prime target is the total cost figure. Since the target figure is expressed as a sales-profit ratio, you must target not only manufacturing costs but also sales and management costs. Fixed costs also play a major role. The main way to reduce fixed costs is by improving work processes.

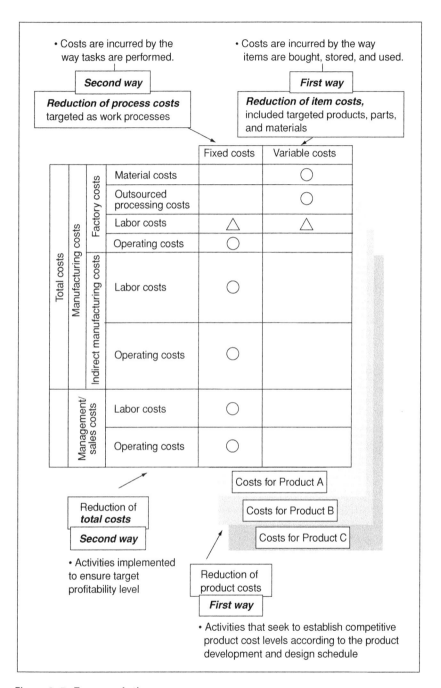

Figure 3-5. Two-way Actions

It is essential that these Cost Half activities cross interdepartmental boundaries, as they are to be undertaken by and for the entire organization.

FIVE TECHNIQUES FOR CHANGING COST-GENERATING SOURCES AND LOCATIONS

One purpose of the Cost Half approach is lowering your cost levels. However, you cannot achieve this merely by pushing existing cost levels downward. Instead, members of your Cost Half activity team need to envision cost levels for products, production processes, and work processes, and then seek to realize them. The activity team also must devise ways of doing business that will help realize a cost structure that generates a high level of profitability. To formulate these visions, they must brainstorm on how to change the cost-generating sources and locations. In the Cost Half business, we refer to these visions as *scenarios*. Figure 3-6 illustrates the process flow from target design to creating cost scenarios. This process flow is an important part of the Cost Half approach—something like its backbone. By following the five major activities in Figure 3-6, the activity team can come up with a Cost Half scenario and then apply Cost Half's five techniques to realize it.

- *Team Activity One: Target design.* The activity team needs to set market-competitive prices and a target profitability rate. Starting from this target value, they next determine the target values for product costs, item costs, and process costs. From the perspective of the team that will be implementing cost-cutting activities for product, item, and process costs, these target values are viewed as *resulting costs*. The team performing these activities set up their activities based on the cost targets that are a result of this target design step.
- *Team Activity Two: Clarify preconditions and restrictions, then set new conditions.* Products, parts, production processes, and work processes are all designed under certain conditions. If you can change these conditions, it becomes easier to change certain cost-generating sources and locations. Usually, the existing conditions have acted as a constraint that confines the scope of suggested activities. The activity team needs to perform in-depth studies to determine whether or not newly established conditions can be applied to existing items, and whether or not restrictions based on the preconditions are valid.

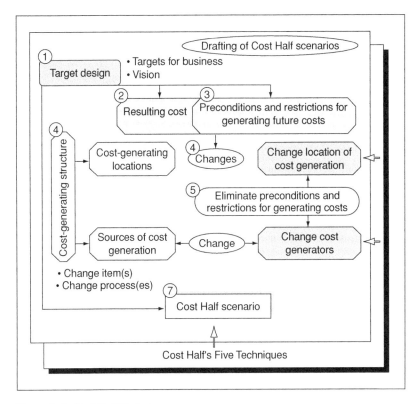

Figure 3-6. Cost Half Techniques

- *Team Activity Three: Analyze cost structures for item costs and process costs.* Under the Cost Half approach, you analyze cost structures in terms of cost-generating sources and locations. Typically, these analyses are performed for individual parts, units, and work tasks. To avoid performing unnecessary analyses, the activity team should consider selecting as targets either items that they view as essential for the "cut by half" orientation described above or those that they view as essential for creating new designs based on the above mentioned "resulting costs."
- *Team Activity Four: Change cost-generating sources and locations.* By "change" we mean establishing something new by eliminating, combining, or replacing the existing thing with something different. Of course, the activity team will give the highest priority to changing cost-generating sources and locations at the same time. Their next-highest priority is to change either cost-generating sources or cost-generating locations. Since

cost generators are interrelated, they will not intentionally decide to change only a source or only a location: instead, they will flexibly plan changes to one or both as the opportunity arises.

- *Team Activity Five: Devise a Cost Half scenario—vision of target.* Members of the activity team can use drawings, flow charts, and the like to illustrate the target product, production process, or work process so that everyone can more easily understand it. Using a simple list of ideas, the team can create a scenario share it with other involved parties.

Once your activity team has completed these five steps, you can begin implementing activities to set up a scenario based on the Cost Half results that they envisioned with their established targets. In other words, the activity team follows these steps in order to set new target values as well as determine which activities are needed to reach them. Each time they go through these steps, they must analyze the structure of cost generators for each target item or process.

Once this is accomplished, you are ready to change the cost-generating structure. Since you analyze the cost-generating structure in terms of interrelated cost-generating *sources* and cost-generating *locations,* you will be changing both. The techniques you will use to achieve this are called *Cost Half's five techniques:*

1. Structural change technique: reduces item costs.
2. Logic change technique: reduces item costs.
3. Process change (PC) technique: reduces process costs.
4. Activity change (AC) technique: reduces process costs.
5. Precondition/restriction change technique: reduces both types of costs.

These five techniques are indispensable for Cost Half implementation, and, as Figure 3-6 shows, they should be included in the training provided to every activity team member who is taking the greedy approach. We will discuss these five techniques in further detail in Chapters 4-6.

THE COST HALF PROGRAM—ACHIEVING LOFTY GOALS

As we just discussed, the Cost Half program consists of a set of well-organized, systematic methods based on three key characteristics for achieving radical cost-reduction goals. We will explain the details of the Cost Half program later; for now, we will briefly examine the overall flow of the program, which consists of five steps.

Step 1: Design the Target

Your Cost Half target should also be a business target, since improvements in business profitability are a key Cost Half strategy. Many companies that have used the Cost Half approach set a target of improving the sales-profit ratio by at least 10 percent. While you can boost profitability by increasing sales, reducing costs, or both, the core idea is to achieve market-competitive product pricing. This means pricing that can be presented as favorable when compared to competing products. Success in this approach adds to the company's sales strength and improves its profitability. Therefore, Cost Half targets originate as business targets that are then developed into targets to be pursued via particular activities.

So the Cost Half approach proceeds from determining target costs to determining the *resulting costs*—the costs that must result from the design of processes, items, and products. This means there is no need to wonder, "How far must we reduce prices?" It also means that any proposed cost reduction idea must ensure that designs for processes and items remain within these "resulting costs" in order to achieve the established target.

Step 2: Analyze Cost-Generating Sources and Locations

First, analyze the characteristics of the item and process costs. By "characteristics" we mean each cost element that goes into the total cost. What type of cost element is it? How does it occur? How does it relate to the item or process? Why does the cost element occur?

Next, you set the *cost emphases* based on the results of the above analysis and then begin investigating the cost-generating sources. In other words, set points of emphasis for achieving the resulting costs; after setting these points, analyze them further in terms of cost-generating sources and locations. This involves more than just making a list of cost-generating sources. You need to ask where the location of each source is. Once you have pinpointed a cost-generating source and its location, you ask: "How can I apply a Cost Half technique to eliminate or otherwise reduce it?" This initiates the next analytical phase.

Since you have already determined cost reduction target values, you must be very careful when studying your means of reaching those targets. For item costs, you might focus on the physical items or locations that incur costs. For process costs, you need to examine the parts of each work process that incur costs. After examining these, you can devise a matrix chart of cost-generating sources and locations to help clarify their interrelations. Each source is likely to relate to several locations. Conversely, it is also common for a single location to be related to several sources, because cost-generating sources and locations interrelate in complex ways that in turn engender costs.

Step 3: Propose Cost Half Measures

Now it is time to come up with some ideas as to how to eliminate or modify cost-generating sources and locations as they appear in your Cost Half matrix chart. Once you have some clear-cut ideas, you're ready to implement them, applying the Cost Half five techniques discussed earlier.

In addition, at the steps where your activity team set targets and analyzed costs, you already have drawn up an outline of the points that need to be emphasized during the Cost Half project. So, with these essential points and Cost Half's five techniques, you can now devise specific measures to implement Cost Half activities.

The steps involved in devising Cost Half measures include:

1. *Confirm* the resulting costs and points of emphasis that were established when setting targets.
2. *Identify* the preconditions and restrictions you used when determining the cost-generating sources and locations.
3. *Analyze* the Cost Half matrix chart.
4. *Devise* Cost Half measures employing Cost Half's five techniques (refer to Figure 3-6 when doing this.)

Also, when compiling the list of cost-generating sources, categorize them according to Cost Half's five techniques. This will help you determine the technique to apply for each cost-generating source, since the various techniques differ in their applicability for certain types of cost-generating sources. So, when analyzing cost-generating locations, examine each thoroughly, ranging from the materials it uses to its completed form. Likewise, when analyzing work processes, examine the entire workflow, then match up all items and processes with costs.

Step 4: Collect the Results of Implementing Cost Half Measures

For this step it is essential that you've implemented the Cost Half measures in systematic, well-organized activities. These measures in turn should have created several implementation strategies, and therefore a lot of activity by the teams in charge of these strategies. One way to make these strategies systematic is to have the teams create scenarios, since each scenario is an image of a process or system to be realized. Then you can form teams around these strategies or around collections of people who relate somehow to the scenario in question. Then, by implementing the Cost Half measures systematically, you can better realize the end state for each scenario. This type of approach will help you avoid the pitfall of making improvements without improving the company organization.

Step 5: Operate a Cost Half Management System

Once you have implemented the Cost Half project and collected results, you can apply the Cost Half management system to the product development process. The knowledge gained through the experience of setting up and implementing a Cost Half project is very valuable indeed. You no longer have to repeat cost-cutting activities using transient, ad-hoc methods, data, and actions because you can build a Cost Half management system to codify the methods you have learned.

The infrastructure of the Cost Half management system works as a set of information systems: one for materials and purchasing, another for processing costs, and yet another for cost management. It is important to implement a Cost Half management system to record and incorporate the experiential knowledge gained by implementing Cost Half activities. Otherwise, your cost-cutting activities are likely to end up like other programs—as transient activities that cannot be easily replicated.

These first three chapters have provided an overview of the Cost Half philosophy. Beginning with Chapter 4 we will enter into a more detailed description of the five Cost Half techniques and how to organize Cost Half projects so you can effectively execute a full-fledged project.

4

Understanding the Cost Half
Promotion System and Techniques

Among all the various theories of methodology, two key aspects are universal: *procedural steps* and *problem-solving techniques.* To strongly promote the Cost Half program, you must not only understand the program but also learn the problem-solving techniques that will move the program forward.

The previous chapters provided an overview of the Cost Half program. Chapters 4 through 7 provide a more detailed description of the five Cost Half techniques as well as how to organize Cost Half projects so you can effectively use these techniques to carry out a full-fledged project. In order to accomplish this, your Cost Half activity members must understand the Cost Half program, learn how to set up an organization for promoting it, and learn how to use various Cost Half techniques. The speed with which your activity teams can implement Cost Half activities, as well as the quality of those activities, depends in part on whether or not they have mastered these fundamentals.

THE CULTIVATION AND ORGANIZATION OF GREEDY MEMBERS

As we saw depicted in Figure 1-4, the leadership and enthusiasm provided by greedy members is essential for successful Cost Half implementation. Cost Half activity members will tend to make the most of their abilities when they are pursuing a theme that is of vital concern to them. Consequently, it is best to begin by assuring that the selected theme is a meaningful one. If it isn't, team members are unlikely to give it their best effort, no matter how dedicated you may be personally to the selected the theme and targets or how many memos are issued by top managers in support of it.

What conditions must you must create to make a project meaningful and interesting to activity members? One condition is that members must be able to envision, based on their previous experiences, the entire road they are about to take in pursuing their selected theme. And they need to know the means by which they will be able to achieve their targets. Consequently, it is important that the course ahead and the means to travel it both are made explicit at the outset.

The training to cultivate greedy members consists of seven clues that work in a cycle of four steps:

1. Preliminary training.
2. Collective training.
3. Mini-OPT (on-the-project training).
4. Course certification.

Each clue and its four steps leads to and opens a door to the Cost Half approach by providing the requisite training for your activity teams. Figure 4-1 shows an example of the seven-clue course for greedy member trainees.

Table 4-1 lists the skills that trainees learn by taking these training courses, which should be set up to last from two to five days.

These skills help the trainee to design a Cost Half vision, set up Cost Half activities, provide the leadership needed to promote those activities, achieve successful results, and—very importantly—implement a regular, ongoing cost management system to sustain the Cost Half Program. Of course, your activity teams refine all of these abilities as they work to implement the Cost Half projects.

The course described in this Figure 4-1 is the one most often taught in Cost Half projects. It provides separate preliminary training for each clue, thus paving the way for the implementation of Cost Half projects.

The training course's schedule is broken into segments so that each clue helps a trainee learn what he or she needs to know early on. It prepares them for the subsequent steps: selecting model parts and model processes, then proceeding with hands-on training.

Course Clue	Objective	Schedule →					
First Clue Study current conditions and design goals.	Learn to set goals	Two days					
Second Clue Study cost generators and locations.	Learn to analyze costs	One day	Two days				
Third Clue Learn techniques to reduce item costs.	Learn to select item cost reduction themes	Two days	Two days				
Fourth Clue Learn techniques to reduce process costs.	Learn to select process cost reduction themes	Two days	Two days				
Fifth Clue Create a scenario. Cost Half actions Management of results	Learn to select Cost Half scenarios and achieve good results				Two days		
Sixth Clue Build and operate a Cost Half cost management system	Learn to build and operate a Cost Half cost management system					Two days	
Seventh Clue Management of Cost Half projects	Learn to manage a Cost Half project as a project leader	Two days					One day

Figure 4–1. A Seven-Clue Course for "Greedy Member" Trainees

Establishing a Cost Half Promotion System

Although some degree of variation exists due to differences among companies, each Cost Half promotion system has the same standard style. Figure 4-2 shows a typical example of a Cost Half promotion organization.

Table 4-1. Skills Learned by Greedy Member Trainees

1. Ability to design targets and desired conditions. Drawing an image of Cost Half results.
2. Ability to utilize Cost Half techniques. Creating a proposal of Cost Half measures.
3. Ability to play the role of Cost Half action team leader. Learning to set new directions for activities.
4. Ability to achieve good results and teach others how to duplicate them. The ability to link successful results to other themes.
5. Ability to build and manage Cost Half's cost management system.

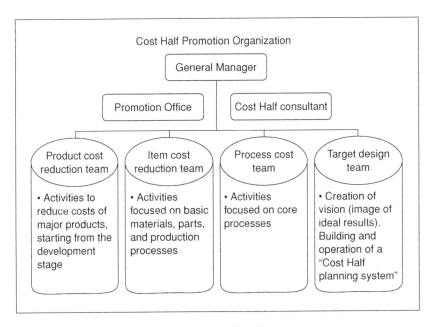

Figure 4-2. Example of Cost Half Promotion Organization

As the figure shows, the Cost Half promotion system includes four teams:

1. Product cost reduction team.
2. Item cost reduction team.
3. Process cost reduction team.
4. Target design team.

As the focus of their cost-cutting activities, the *product cost reduction team* selects products just entering the development stage.

This helps coordinate Cost Half activities with product development activities.

The *item cost reduction team* and *process cost reduction team* both carry out activities that contribute to higher profitability. In contrast to the product cost reduction team, which focuses on products that are currently under development and will not be marketed for at least a year, these two teams implement activities that target the overall direct and indirect management of products already on the market.

The *target design team* works mainly on devising targets, but also studies trends used to predict results of activities in progress. This team also contributes to building and operating a cost management system once the activities have been completed.

It is essential also to establish a promotion office that facilitates the progress of each team's activities. Furthermore, it is necessary to assign someone to bear overall responsibility as the general manager of Cost Half activities. Meanwhile, it is the Cost Half consultant's role to provide various kinds of tangible support from the earliest stages of the Cost Half activities and to work cooperatively with the four teams. Each team should consist of members who have learned how to analyze problems and propose solutions, plus a leader who has completed the greedy training described above. Tables 4-2 and 4-3 list some precautions and other key points of advice regarding the set-up of a Cost Half promotion system.

The main precautionary message of Table 4-2 is that it takes a strong leader to put together a team in his or her spare time, and without such leadership the team's activities are likely to extend over a long period of time. That is why it is so important to have an effective promotion system for these activities. Attempts to organize teams without such a promotion system are like attempts to chase two rabbits at once—the end result is that both rabbits get away.

Table 4-3 presents a list of several key points to keep in mind during these activities. Regarding point 2 ("Set appropriate target values"), bear in mind that the general idea is to set a goal of cutting costs by approximately half. There is a difference between a necessary target and an activity target: the former is a minimum level that must be achieved, while the latter is a standard that the activities and improvement proposals aim to achieve. There have been cases when neither target is reached, but in those cases even the minimum target is set very high.

Table 4-2. Establishing a Cost Half Promotion System: Precautions

1. A promotion system that is not well planned is ultimately just a waste.
2. Unless the people involved are especially brilliant, it is counterproductive to assign several roles to the same person.
3. Cost reduction is specialized work, and specialists are needed to implement cost reduction activities swiftly.
4. Once people have climbed the ladder of training and reached the rooftop of activities, it is best to kick away the ladder.

Table 4-3. Establishing a Cost Half Promotion: Key Points

Point 1: Be careful and thorough in selecting cost reduction themes and their requirements.	It is especially important to do a thorough job of selecting the goals you want to achieve because your cost reduction themes will be oriented toward these goals. Next, you must determine the requirements for implementing the cost reduction themes. In short, to discover the best means for achieving your goals, you must first carefully and thoroughly identify your cost reduction themes and their requirements.
Point 2: Set appropriate target values.	Obviously, when it comes to cost reduction, the greater the reduction the better. However, bigger cost cuts necessarily involve bigger changes in current conditions, and it takes a correspondingly bigger cost-cutting push to effect such changes. That is why it is crucial to carefully and studiously set appropriate target values.
Point 3: Address all relevant costs.	When setting targets for cost-cutting activities, it is important to include all costs that contribute to the total target cost. When you leave out any of these relevant costs, you must cut the rest of the costs even more to achieve the total cost target. If the target cost reduction is especially challenging, those other costs may not be able to absorb the difference. Besides, the best way to strengthen the organization as a whole is to address *all* relevant costs.
Point 4: To understand costs, you must understand the cost generators.	Understanding costs is an essential precondition for launching effective cost-cutting activities. Generally, you cannot understand costs simply by examining the various expenses incurred by factories and offices. In all too many cases, cost-cutting teams mistakenly believe they understand costs when they have a fairly complete list of such expenses, even though they do not understand the cost generators (cost sources). It may be easy enough to grasp the cost generators for products manufactured completely in-house, but there are other cost generators that you need to understand. In fact, you must get a handle on *all* cost generators if you want to be sure of selecting good themes that will help you achieve your cost reduction targets.

(*continued*)

Table 4-3. Establishing a Cost Half Promotion: Key Points (*continued*)

Point 5: Clarify the reasons for cost reductions.	Radical cost reductions require radical measures. Sometimes, these radical measures require major changes in company policy, a rechanneling of resources, or even a reorganization of the network of vendors—all of which call for high-level decision-making. The criterion for taking such drastic steps is whether or not the resulting changes will create the kinds of conditions needed for the desired cost reductions. Unless you clearly state the reasons why they are required, the will to make such radical changes is likely to wither away in face of strong resistance or other difficulties.
Point 6: Expect the unexpected and don't give up.	After you make improvements, a survey of the actual conditions never quite corresponds to the conditions conceived in the proposed improvements. Various obstacles invariably appear to prevent realization of the conceptual goals. The reports generated on desktops typically fail to account for several factors, and this tends to put a limit on successful implementation. Consequently, it takes great perseverance to achieve the envisioned results. In fact, *every member* of each cost reduction team—not just the leaders—must be determined to "hang in there." Naturally, the goals must be appropriate (that is, achievable), but even then it takes bold perseverance to successfully carry out the implementation process.

THE FIVE COST HALF TECHNIQUES

Let us now examine the five Cost Half techniques that we've been referring to since Chapter 1. Some of these techniques focus on reducing item costs; others focus on reducing process costs, which typically requires changes in current systems, materials, structures, and work procedures. *The five Cost Half techniques are the instruments of change.* Figure 4-3 illustrates the way in which these five techniques interface with item costs and processes.

Let's begin by considering the basic, conventional approaches that companies have been taking when designing products and production processes. Obviously, these approaches vary from company to company, even when they are using similar techniques and equipment.

Changes in Preconditions and Limitations

Many cost generators are related to a company's basic approach and techniques. The Cost Half approach considers a company's existing

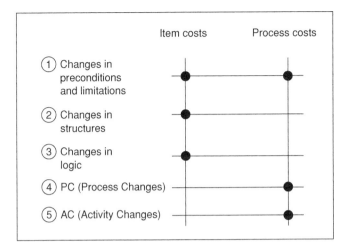

Figure 4-3. Five Cost Half Techniques

preconditions, and the limitations based on those preconditions, to be the foundation of that company's current way of doing things. When a company is stuck in its current preconditions and limitations, it is hard to get "outside the box" when proposing improvements—and that in itself is a cost generator. Such a company is not able to embrace the essential fact that it must re-invent itself to meet the demands of the changing market environment. Accordingly, the first of the five Cost Half techniques focuses on *making changes in preconditions and limitations.*

Changes in Structures

The elements that are combined in products and production include parts and work processes. The term *structures* refer to these constituent elements and the way they are combined. Ordinarily, these structures are devised on an ad-hoc basis, in response to trends in sales volume, production yield, market needs, or requests from customers. As a result of these ad-hoc structures, measures are devised and implemented on an "as needed" basis. Consequently, they are based on a variety of orientations and do not follow any one basic orientation.

Such an approach is clearly inadequate in terms of efficiency and as a cost-cutting strategy. It is not even based on principles that you can call logical or particularly effective. This approach leaves ample room for cost generators to arise and become the accepted norm.

A company can gain a new perspective by changing the elements that comprise its structures. Take purchasing-related structures, for example. The elements in these structures include where and how you purchase items and how much you pay for them. The goal is to find the most advantageous purchase arrangements among those offered by the many available vendors. A company can also change the way it uses constituent elements such as parts, processes, vendors, and subcontractors; for instance, by changing the quantities and/or types of elements in the configuration. In sum, this approach, which focuses mainly on reducing item costs, is behind the second of the five techniques—*making changes in structures.*

Changes in Logic

For designers and production engineers, as the persons responsible for overseeing and aiding the teams' progress, the solution to a problem often cannot be devised simply by isolating that problem. Instead, they generally arrive at solutions by trying out several different ideas until the correct approach becomes clear.

For example, how would one find a solution for the problem of having to increase an engine's output while reducing its consumption of oil? First, one would have to examine the issue of friction among the engine's various moving parts. This would include the gears, crankshaft assembly, and pistons. Let us focus on the pistons. The first thing to consider is how precisely the pistons and cylinders fit together. You must also consider the elliptical shape of the pistons, as well as the number of piston rings and their shape. Finally, you would have to actually run the engine to study how these parts are functioning.

Even after a solution is found from the designer's perspective, you would have to determine whether or not the designer's solution can be implemented in the manufacturing processes, which requires testing and verification at the processes themselves.

Thus, you can take many paths to solve any given problem. For the problem-solver, it is a question of choosing the most appropriate path for the task at hand. To select this path, Cost Half uses what might be called *design logic*. Sometimes this logic is based on standards for selecting among options, and sometimes it is based simply on experience and intuition. And that is where problems arise. What happens when the standards include only performance and functional standards is clear; it is also clear that without any cost standards or cost perspective, cost generators remain hidden. There is surely a need to change the design logic so that it explicitly includes consideration of cost generators. And so we have our third of the five Cost Half techniques–*changes in logic*.

Process Change

Business activities include more than just some method of "work." In reality, business activity takes shape as a process, becoming part of the entire flow of work, from where it begins to where it ends. At the very least, many types of work go into a given business activity.

Since business activity is really a process, the way it is initiated has a huge impact on the direction taken and the end results. Any mess made early on inevitably must be cleaned up at some point downstream. When the process is a prolonged one, there is consequently some duplication of work at later stages. At the outset, since you cannot envision the entire process, it is as if you are facing a high wall that stands between you and the downstream stages, and you must blindly send work over the wall without seeing where it is going. The wall is a major obstacle for people at upstream and downstream stages, who should be gaining feedback from each other that will help to spark some new ideas. As it stands, a company that does not scrutinize its processes cannot design a profitable flow of business activity. This not only allows but encourages the creation of numerous cost generators.

Consider the product development process, for instance. What happens when the constituent elements of a product are not identified at an early stage in the product development process, such as the stage at which the basic design concepts are established? What happens if the product design is unfinished? The gap left by a lack of completeness must be filled somehow at the design stage. And if no one even recognizes the gap as such, the final product concept is sure to be less than complete.

If you allow incomplete product designs to be carried forward, then products based on incomplete designs will become the norm for your company. To take a different approach that includes a complete array of constituent elements, you must change the overall design of the product. This, of course, gives rise to more cost generators. The Cost Half techniques used to address these problems are collectively called *process change (PC) techniques*.

Activity Change

You can categorize business activities in terms of their various qualities. When you do this, you'll find that many types of business activities do not directly produce the expected output. In fact, about 70 percent of them fall into this category. In other words, only about 30 percent of business activities are directly tied to desired results. People who have trouble believing this need only conduct a work sampling study to confirm it.

In any case, you must consider this as a cost-generating factor. It stands to reason, then, that by addressing this issue you can increase the ratio of business activities that are more effective in directly producing the expected output. The Cost Half techniques used to do deal with this are collectively called *activity change (AC) techniques.*

Cost Half Techniques and Various Business Activities

Figure 4-4 illustrates the relationship between the five Cost Half techniques and various types of business activities that take place in product development processes and production supply processes.

The starting point for a product is the market and customers for whom the product is intended. Companies translate customer needs into product concepts or, conversely, companies propose product concepts to customers. Both of these processes are influenced by the company's habitual ways of thinking and by a variety of preconditions and limitations. In particular, problems occur unless the company strikes a balance between its product concepts and specifications and the constraints imposed by the need for competitive pricing.

When translating product concepts and specifications into product structures, which is a core part of the design process, various cost generators are introduced, including generators of both item costs and process costs. Another aspect of the product design process is the determination of part specifications and uses, which comprises an early upstream stage in the flow of business activities. The quality of business activities at this early stage makes an immense difference in determining the quality of business activities at later stages.

In Chapters 5 through 7, we will look in greater detail at the five Cost First techniques. The many figures relating to these techniques you will encounter in these chapters will illustrate how some of these cost generators are created. It is important to apply the Cost Half techniques as they relate to item cost generators that occur at and between information process stages, such as when translating product concept

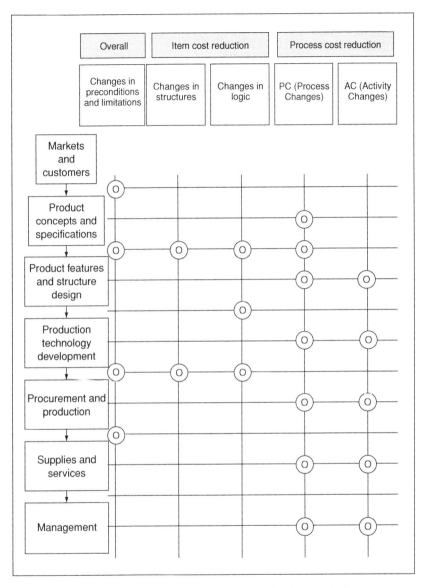

Figure 4-4. The Product Development Process, the Production Supply Process, and the Five Cost Half Techniques

information for use in the design of product structures. This is because it is precisely at these between-stage points of information processing, that process cost generators tend to be created. Finally, you tend to create cost generators by the very manner in which you carry out your work. With the Cost Half techniques you can revolutionize how work is done, and thus effectively control your process cost generators.

5

Cost Half Technique 1: Changes in Preconditions and Limitations

As mentioned in Chapter 4, products, production systems, and various work processes are all rooted in certain preconditions—in a company's way of doing business, its production processes, and its business activities. These preconditions cause products that have the same functions for the same markets to differ simply because they are made by different companies. As a result of the various experiences, experiments, and tests conducted within the framework of these preconditions, each company establishes limitations on what it is willing to do, and builds both products and production systems on the foundation of these preconditions. A company's particular preconditions—the requirements it must meet to design and build products—are also shaped by its history and attitude toward customer service.

Meanwhile, the company's limitations—which are restrictive conditions it places upon product development and its scope of activities—are largely shaped by past customer complaints and the company's product testing results. It takes a brave company to step back and detach itself from its limitations. Typically, employees resign themselves to plodding onward without questioning their company's self-imposed limitations.

In the final analysis, it is those in charge who establish and maintain preconditions and limitations as a result of their conventional way of thinking. Only by changing their mindset can they target and change the company's preconditions and limitations. This in turn will facilitate changes in the ideas and approaches behind the company's products, production systems, work processes, and design methods. Only by making bold and sweeping changes can you uncover and address those areas where cost generators reside.

TARGETING AND CHANGING PRODUCT PRECONDITIONS AND LIMITATIONS

To develop new products, companies elucidate and translate customers' requirements into product specifications. Product planners develop these specifications by asking how they can reflect each customer's needs in building new products. Then the company goes about its particular way of translating these customer needs into product specifications. This product development stage is where a company's preconditions and limitations have their main impact.

Figure 5-1 illustrates how you can represent preconditions and limitations in a relatively simple format for analysis. The product in this example is a sealing material that is used for soundproofing and moisture-proofing. This product is formed via a process of rubber extrusion, and it involves high material costs.

One of the customer requirements is for a larger contact surface on these seals. However, an unrestrained attempt to meet this requirement would drive costs much higher. The product designers looked for a more promising new material but were unable to find one. The inexpensive materials were all unsatisfactory for soundproofing and moisture-proofing. They also tried making improvements in the extrusion process to reduce costs, but failed in that attempt also.

Finally, they did an analysis of the preconditions and limitations. They noted all of the information related to product specifications in a product specification manual and in an extrusion specification manual. In the process, they came across a precondition that required "use of uniform materials." They were well aware of this precondition and had always taken pains to meet it. Yet this was exactly where they had reached an impasse.

So they conducted a new analysis at that point and asked the basic questions—when, why, and how?—to determine the basis for that precondition. They had no answer for the last question, nor could anyone remember who had mandated this precondition or for what

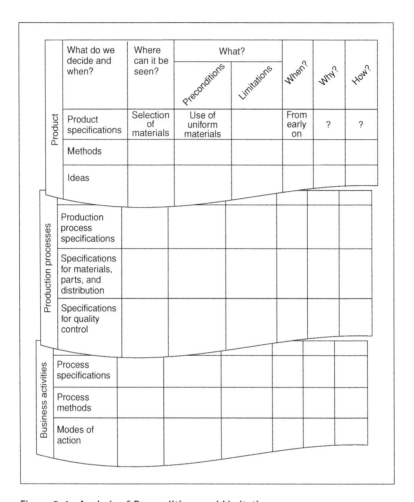

Figure 5-1. Analysis of Preconditions and Limitations

reason. The designers thus tried a new approach: they changed the precondition that stated they could use only uniform (i.e., simple) materials.

It turned out that the only reason for using uniform materials was to ensure suitability for soundproofing and moisture-proofing. Therefore, as long as the same purpose could be served, the designers figured that it would be OK to use compound materials instead of simple ones. They started studying various compounds of inexpensive and expensive materials that could serve this purpose. The result was that they did find compounds that would enable a dramatic reduction in material costs. The designers then tested the compounds to see if they met the customer requirements, and indeed found some that did. This demonstrates the importance of the Cost Half technique of changing preconditions and limitations—a point underscored by the fact that the impact of preconditions and limitations increases at the later stages of product development.

Once the designers had identified the proper compounds, their next step was to analyze the selection of manufacturing methods that suited the product specifications. You must consider many constraints when selecting manufacturing methods. In addition to the product specifications, the structural design parameters to be determined at the next step—including not only size and weight but also operability, handling convenience, and various design features—will be influenced in many ways by the selected manufacturing method. Accordingly, many preconditions and limitations are inherent in the decision-making process that determines the selection of materials and the structure of parts.

After clarifying target products and parts, it is time to analyze the conceptual process of product design. Here again it is important to flush out preconditions and limitations that are inherent in this conceptual process. Of course, it is not necessary to flush out the preconditions and limitations for every single part. Instead, we should select the most important and necessary parts and analyze those.

TARGETING AND CHANGING PRODUCTION PROCESS PRECONDITIONS AND LIMITATIONS

Product specifications, manufacturing methods, and structural design also significantly impact production processes. Basically, at this stage, product developers must decide how they will link production processes to build the product under development. When considering preconditions and limitations at the level of production processes, product developers must first ask themselves how product specifications and structures function as conditions. From the Cost Half perspective, you must ask, "How can these factors be hypothesized as affecting production processes?"

Also, many preconditions and limitations occur from the perspective of production engineering. For example, there is typically a precondition to the effect that "this type of equipment has always been the equipment we have used." Likewise, there are usually some fixed ideas about the sequence of production processes, such as "this process has always come after that process." In many cases these assumptions and fixed ideas were established in response to previous situations concerning orders, production yields, and product models under production at the time. People who invested their time and trouble in establishing them now maintain them as an entrenched system in the hope that they will prevent problems. What arises is a manufacturing organization in which people are kept busy maintaining the status quo through daily quality and production yield checks and management of storage and delivery, and do not take the time to devise any major changes or pursue innovative ideas.

Another factor to recognize as a precondition or limitation is that it is hard to propose major changes for a large production system because the system's sheer size means such changes take a lot of time. So companies tend to settle for making incremental improvements instead. Consider, as an example, a distribution system that moves goods to and from the factory as well as within it. Typically, such a distribution system includes a parts supply system whereby materials and parts intended for machining or assembly processes are first moved into a warehouse and later conveyed to the production line as they are needed. Such systems are usually long established and, over the years, fine-tuned by many small improvements. Furthermore, employees basically accept these systems without question as a precondition for how the company circulates parts and materials. This often holds true both for distribution systems that send parts and materials into and out of factories, and for systems that convey parts and materials within factories.

In addition, there are many preconditions and limitations inherent in the systems used by affiliated companies and vendors who are located at a distance from the main manufacturing company and have little daily contact with them. All of these long-established systems need to be reexamined from a fresh perspective so you can identify the existing preconditions and limitations. After that, you can come up with new proposals for ways to change the limitations that affect product design factors and production engineering factors. A company must accept the challenge of overcoming past limitations based on the size of the production system or on whether or not the object in question is handled in-house or elsewhere. Instead, it must create a new set of requirements for process design based on new concepts and new methods of cost reduction.

In fact, it is essential that your organization makes it a habit to accept such challenges.

TARGETING AND CHANGING BUSINESS ACTIVITY PRECONDITIONS AND LIMITATIONS

We are easily able to view products and production processes as objects, which makes it easy to tell when they have changed. By contrast, business activities are centered on people and have no visible shape or form in the way an object does. It takes some effort to make business activities visible, but the effort is worthwhile, since the "invisible areas" are where many preconditions and limitations reside and grow over the years.

Also, because people are at the center of business activities, they constitute an area of improvement-making that some of us are loath to wade into. Even though they recognize the need for logical thinking, it is very hard for people to change work processes if they perceive that doing so poses a threat to their authority. Making such changes therefore generally requires strong support from top management.

The preconditions and limitations to be targeted and changed include work processes (i.e., the links between business activities), process systems, and modes of action or behavior. In particular, given the truism that "wherever there are people, there are business activities," it is important to learn to identify work processes *in general* as well as *specific* work processes. The first step is to select the target work processes. Next, you must examine the target work processes with a view toward changing them. You can do this using check and control functions that help flush out the preconditions and limitations that divert the work processes from directly serving their intended purpose. At the same time, you must also seek to flush out work processes that are overly time-consuming. You need to be on the lookout for tasks that, like a muddy marsh, always take longer than expected to get through.

CHANGING THE BACKGROUND FACTORS CAUSING THE PRECONDITIONS AND LIMITATIONS

Once you have flushed out the preconditions and limitations, it will be immediately apparent that you need to change them, and you will have little difficulty in arguing that this is so. Since the mere existence of such preconditions and limitations is a problem, the solution begins with *completely* eliminating them, which means it is important to address the background factors that gave rise to them.

		Background factors	
		Undefined	Defined
Causal factors	Conditions inside company	1	2
	Conditions outside of company	2	3

1: Changes in preconditions and limitation are indispensable
2: Study of changes in preconditions and limitations
3: Detailed study of changes in preconditions and limitations

Figure 5-2. Analysis of Necessity and Possibility of Changing Preconditions
          and Limitations

Figure 5-1 provides a good way to approach this by asking the basic questions (when, why, and how). Also, you can develop a matrix like the one in Figure 5-2 to study background factors and causal factors.

When a precondition or limitation is at level 1, it must be eliminated or changed. When it is at level 2, it must be changed for a particular purpose. When it is at level 3, the causes are clearly identified and you should study them from another perspective.

Now that you have begun identifying the areas where you need to completely change the way your firm does things, you are clearly on the road to making further changes. This leads us to Chapter 6 and Cost Half technique two, Changes in Structures.

....

6

....

Cost Half Technique 2:
Changes in Structures

The first thing to realize when using structural change techniques is that *costs are numbers*. The question is, "What *kind* of numbers?" In a manufacturing company, these numbers represent parts spread around the factory, dies and equipment units on the factory floor, or computers, printers, or fax machines in an office. The number of these objects tends to increase without our even realizing it. Moreover, when you face a growing number of objects, it takes more people to manage them. In other words, as the amount of work increases so does the number of consumable supplies, spare parts, and so on. Things generally get bigger and more complicated—all of which adds up to higher costs.

Many managers believe that when production output and sales volume are steadily increasing, you can allow these numbers to grow without causing problems. They figure the rise in production output and sales will cover the rise in cost-related numbers. *But costs are not merely a matter of numbers!* It's really all about the *control* of these numbers, and the whole organization suffers when costs are not continuously controlled. Before anyone realizes it, costs everywhere are increasing needlessly.

"If costs are numbers, then we should seek to reduce numbers." This is the variety reduction program (VRP) philosophy that was publicized in a book published about 15 years ago by the Japan Management

Association (*Variety Reduction Program,* 1984). Many VRP projects have been implemented since then and, sure enough, a reduction in numbers (in terms of variety of parts, for example) has typically resulted in a reduction in costs. The Cost Half techniques adopt this approach but widen the scope of target numbers. Accordingly, the VRP approach is reflected in the Cost Half technique for changing structures.

PERSPECTIVE ONE: COSTS AS NUMBERS

First, let us consider the kinds of numbers you need to reduce in order to change structures. In this context, *structure* refers not only to an entity but also to the set of interdependent relationships among the elements that configure the entity. To understand these relationships in a structure's costs, you must clearly identify the various constituent elements. The Cost Half approach focuses on two types of constituent elements:

1. Types and quantities of parts that go into products.
2. Types and quantities of individual production processes that go into the production system.

You cannot effectively lower item costs unless you change the structure of both types of constituent elements.

Now let's examine the structure changes in the product and production process that is illustrated in Figure 6-1. As can be seen in the figure, the product structure changes included plans for reducing the variety and quantity of parts and for simplifying both products and production processes. Through this approach, the manufacturer intended to make further progress in factory automation even while implementing variety reduction. They planned to reduce part variety by increasing the number of fixed components and establishing more common components among different products. They also sought to make parts more multifunctional and intensive in order to reduce their number.

The effectiveness of this plan depends upon boosting efficiency and automation in production processes. The manufacturer also plans to achieve a number of other product structure changes through ongoing, consistent implementation of these types of activities.

Establishing the Fixed and Variable Approach

Most manufacturing companies deal with a wide variety of products, so it is important that they find ways to increase the share of

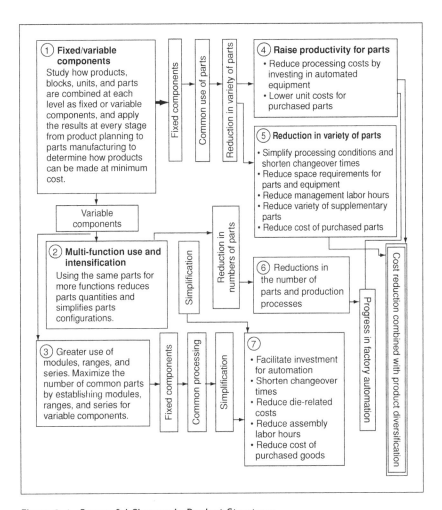

Figure 6-1. Successful Changes in Product Structures

fixed components used among their many types of products, parts, and processes. Having a wide variety of products is only natural, seeing as those products must meet diverse customer requirements. With a wide variety of products you can also expect a wide variety of parts. However, unnecessary costs can arise depending on how parts are managed and used. When the number and variety of parts increases, so does the time required to manufacture and manage them (this includes parts purchased from outside vendors). In other words, the assortment of product specifications and management processes expands.

To cut costs, you need to increase the number of common parts that you can use in several different product models that have similar specifications. Specifications cannot be too similar, though, because customers demand variety. The key to resolving this dilemma is to sort components into fixed and variable components. The components that must be different to meet differing customer needs are the variable components; those that you can use in several different product models are the fixed components. We might also refer to the fixed components as *common components*. It is important, however, to have a policy against using common components carelessly, at the expense of product diversification.

Whenever reasonable, you should laterally deploy this policy of using common components to part/product specifications and production processes. It is particularly effective to deploy the common components policy differently for different product grades, because higher-grade products are typically designed more specifically to meet certain customer needs than are lower-grade products. This means that you can clarify how variable components should be used based on an analysis of the needs for each product grade.

Under the common components policy, all components that do not have to be variable components should, in principle, be fixed components. You should group both variable components and common components according to their size, subassembly units, and the types of products in which they are used. You should plan for common uses of fixed components whenever possible. The end result will be a reduction in the variety of parts. At the same time, we should seek to automate or otherwise reduce labor requirements at the production points where these parts are processed or assembled. Having a smaller variety of parts also simplifies the management of part purchases.

Furthermore, you can help minimize variable components by applying the multifunction use and intensification approach, described later. You also should strive to simplify structures and production processes and reduce changeover-related labor requirements.

In addition, it is a good idea to set regulations concerning the use of variable components and to establish modules, ranges, and series of parts, as is illustrated in the following table and figures. This approach will help to simplify processing conditions and thereby serve to lower costs incurred at production processes. The gist of changing structures is an unflagging effort to establish fixed

Table 6-1. The Fixed/Variable Approach

1. *Establish a variety of products that are all combinations of fixed components (base parts for a product series) and variable components (base parts for specific product models).* Variable components exist mainly to meet market needs. Fixed components exist mainly to meet production needs.
2. *Establish fixed components and flexible processes.* While establishing variable components to meet needs for diverse specifications, establish fixed components as thoroughly rationalized components. Likewise, manufacturing processes must be established as flexible processes with high productivity.
3. *Fixed components.* Find out how many of a product group's parts can be shared as common components, and try to manufacture the common components using just one or only a few production processes. Also, seek to automate or further mechanize processes to reduce labor requirements.
4. *Variable components.* Variable components are used to meet the individual needs of certain types of products. Most of the production processes for these components will involve some manual labor, but you still can apply automation and mechanization for control purposes.

components whenever possible. Table 6-1 summarizes the fixed/variable approach.

Figure 6-2 illustrates a simple case example for electric fans to help clarify how to use an approach that distinguishes between fixed and variable components.

In this example, the designations of fixed and variable extend all the way to the specifications, performance characteristics, and structure of the product and its parts. As a result, the company was able to reduce processing labor hours a full 70 percent while cutting die costs about 65 percent. These impressive results sprang from efforts made in the following areas.

- The company thoroughly considered the product characteristics that were needed to meet specific customer needs.
- They explicitly used variable components to provide these product characteristics. They even organized the variable components into pattern-based groups rather than dealing with them in a piecemeal fashion.
- They made maximum use of fixed components, especially at pre-assembly processes. This helped to make the assembly processes more efficient as well. When upstream processes become more orderly, the flow of work at downstream processes becomes more efficient.
- They took full advantage, overall, of die-based manufacturing and automation technologies.

Case Study of Fixed
Components and Variable
Components

Sort components into fixed components and variable components, and try to establish as many components as possible as fixed components (components shared in a series of products).

Fixed components	Variable components	Evaluation		
		Performance	Productivity	Market needs
Width and depth	Height	O	O	O
Height and depth	Width	O	✕	✕
Height and width	Depth	✕	△	✕

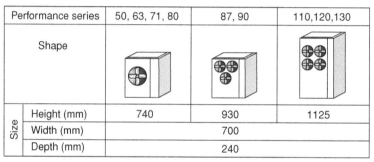

Performance series	50, 63, 71, 80	87, 90	110,120,130
Shape			
Height (mm)	740	930	1125
Width (mm)	700		
Depth (mm)	240		

(Size)

Effects

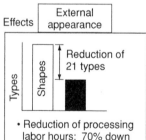

External appearance

Reduction of 21 types

Types / Shapes

• Reduction of processing labor hours: 70% down
• Reduction of die costs: About 65% down

Key points
1. Products continue to meet customer needs with relevant features
2. Size variations (in width, height, diameter, etc.) are organized into patterns
3. More fixed components at pre-assembly processes
4. Better die investments, more automation, and better economies of scale

Figure 6-2. Case Study of Fixed Components and Variable Components

Applying the Fixed/Variable Principle to Products and Production Process Simultaneously

Refer to Figure 6-3, which also relates to the fixed/variable distinction—specifically, how you can apply the fixed/variable component principle to products and production processes at the same time.

Ordinarily, processing-related activities (machining, die-casting, etc.) are set up separately for the various product types. This means that there are about as many processing production lines as there are modular unit designations. In the lower half of Figure 6-3, we see how these modular units are reorganized under the principle of fixed components. The units that involve fixed components all fall under

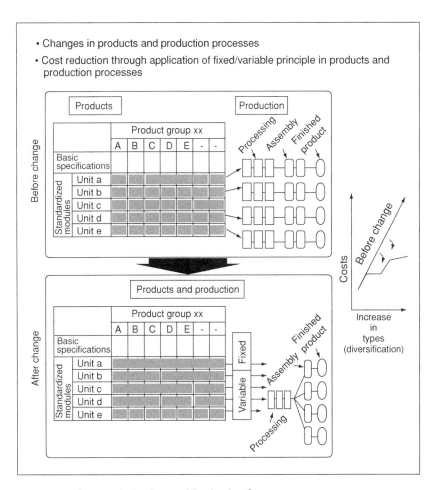

Figure 6-3. Changes in Product and Production Structures

patterns of one to three product type combinations. This enables processing-related activities to be fixed within one production line, resulting in large savings in processing-related costs.

By applying the fixed/variable component principle to assembly processes, the company was able to enhance its automation of assembly work. It was also able to establish subprocesses and intensive assembly processes parallel to the main assembly line. As Figure 6-3 shows, establishing fixed product specifications contributes much to the rationalization of production processes. In other words, applying the fixed/variable principle paves the way for cost-saving changes in the entire production system. There would be no point in applying this principle if it was not effective for this purpose.

The Multifunction Use and Intensification Approach

It is only natural that you use fixed components when investigating ways to reduce the number of product parts and production processes. Variable components, though, are intended to serve particular customer requirements, and if they are used individually in structure designs for various products they tend to increase rather than reduce variety, and therefore increase costs. By their nature, variable components also tend to require more work in terms of production engineering. Consequently, it should come as no surprise that more work is needed to apply the principles of multifunction use and intensification to variable components for the sake of reducing the number of parts and production processes. The *multifunction* aspect of this approach is a design methodology that seeks to make one part serve several functions to enable a reduction in the number of parts. The *intensification* aspect is another design methodology that seeks to group parts together into structures. Table 6-2 summarizes the multifunction use and intensification approach.

Of course, you can use this approach for other things besides parts, such as production processes. This approach is generally used to trim down structures. As was indicated in Table 6-2, it begins by eliminating surplus or superfluous specifications. The example shown in Figure 6-4 represents a simple application of this approach. Here, two functions have been integrated into one part to reduce the number of required parts. Since this requires fewer purchased parts, there is a percent reduction in purchased parts costs. You can devise such innovations by challenging the status quo and the traditional way of doing things, thoroughly considering how functions can be intensified.

Table 6-2. Multifunction Use and Intensification Approach

Multifunction use and intensification approach. A technique that reduces the number of parts and production processes by implementing the desired functions using a minimum of parts and a simple structure. This technique is applied in four areas.

1. *Application in terms of specifications and functions.* Eliminate surplus or superfluous specifications
2. *Application in terms of functions.* Use the same part for several functions, and use the same process for several functions
3. *Application in terms of structures.* Reduce several parts to one common part and several processes to one common process
4. *Simplification of parts and reduction of material costs.* Simplify processes and reduce labor hours.

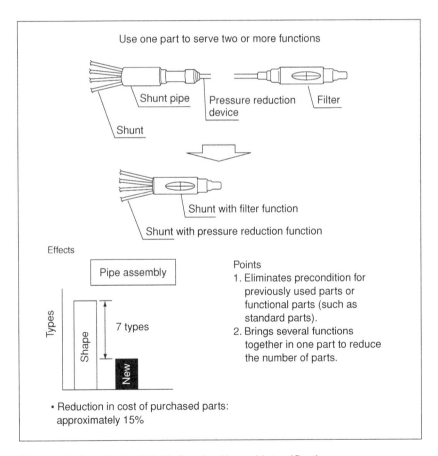

Figure 6-4. Case Study of Multi-function Use and Intensification

You might wonder, "But doesn't it cost more in the end to design and build parts with multiple functions?" Not necessarily, but it is not simply a matter of combining several parts into one part. Instead, the aim is to design an entirely new part that serves all of the intended functions. The net result is a reduction in cost generators.

Using the perspective of "costs as numbers," Figure 6-5 summarizes the approach to changing product and production structures. The figure begins with products at the top and moves to production processes below. It shows how having more types and numbers of parts requires that you have more production processes—all of which are cost generators. Figure 6-5 shows a way of breaking down these

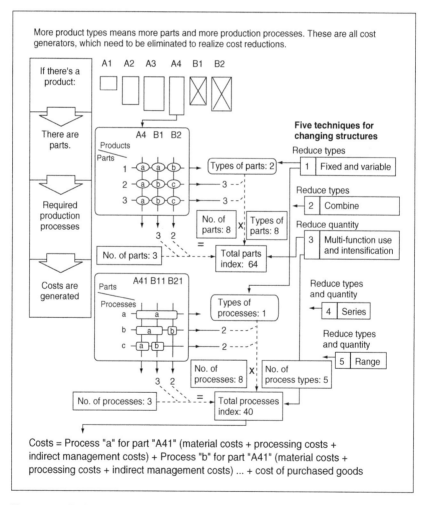

Figure 6-5. Techniques for Changes in Structures: ① Changes in Product Structures

cost generators by providing indexes, one for types and other for quantities. These are then multiplied to produce a *total parts index*. Likewise for production processes, you multiply the types and quantities of production processes to arrive at a *total process index*.

Past experience shows that if you can reduce both of these index values by about half, manufacturing costs will be cut by approximately 30 percent. To achieve such a result, you use such techniques as the fixed/variable principle and multifunction use and intensification.

PERSPECTIVE TWO: COSTS ARRANGED IN STRUCTURES

In the previous section, we discussed the perspective of costs as numbers. But since costs also depend on how items and processes are arranged, Cost Half takes a second perspective when applying techniques to change cost structures—how costs are *arranged* in structures. In particular, there are three types of cost structures.

1. Production site structures.
2. In-house/outside manufacturing structures.
3. Purchasing structures.

We will now discuss how you can apply Cost Half techniques to change these cost structures.

Changes in Production Site Structures

Expansion of product types, production yields, and consumer markets has encouraged a strategy of moving production sites to locations that offer cost advantages. However, over the long term, this strategy often provides a breeding ground for various cost generators.

For example, at some of these relocated factories, the operating rate takes a downturn. Meanwhile, new products are being introduced to shore up the business. This exposes problems that are due to different production system levels; that is, the production system is more advantageous for some products than for others. It also makes the distribution system more complicated. In addition, there are added indirect costs for managing the widening range of products. There are two principles you can effectively apply to change these kinds of cost generators: the fixed/variable principle and the *coherency principle.*

For instance, consider a company that has adopted a basic policy of lowering prices, which means they are concentrating on products that they can make inexpensively. To do that, they focus on low-cost

items. These items become the company's fixed components. Therefore, they know they will need to build the kind of production system that is most effective for keeping prices down. However, they
anticipate a need for product diversification, so they also must focus
on some products that can flexibly meet various customer requirements. To the extent that such flexibility is important, the company
needs to build a production system adaptable enough to involve
numerous variable components. Now they are ready to select a production site that will be suitable for the particular characteristics of
their focus on repeated use of components and grouping of similar
types of components.

The coherency principle requires a functional overlapping of production and sales components, including new product development
and supply processes. Functions that overlap should be concentrated
at one location. Thus, we can change cost generators by changing
the allocation for production items and business activity functions.

Figure 6-6 illustrates the steps involved when we study the structure of production sites. The first step is to flush out cost generators.
Next, we analyze these cost generators and their locations. These
steps are helpful later on when we seek to apply the fixed/variable
principle and the coherency principle.

Changes in In-House/Outside Manufacturing Structure

The proper way to address in-house/outside manufacturing issues
depends upon the locations of technology and cost priorities. Often,
the decision whether to manufacture in-house or use an outside con-
tractor depends on which works better for ensuring adequate production output. The Cost Half approach analyzes the production
processes related to the parts or units that you are targeting in order
to achieve desired cost levels. After studying these processes with a
view toward multifunction use and intensification, you must ask
whether certain processes would be better concentrated in-house or
at an outside manufacturer.

In the example in Figure 6-7, the company had been purchasing
key parts from outside vendors but was able to bring production of
those parts in-house using its own engineering. Naturally, this gave
them a cost advantage. Another good reason to establish in-house
manufacturing of key parts is that such parts can help establish a
competitive advantage in new product development. The company
in this case study also set up subassembly processes parallel to the

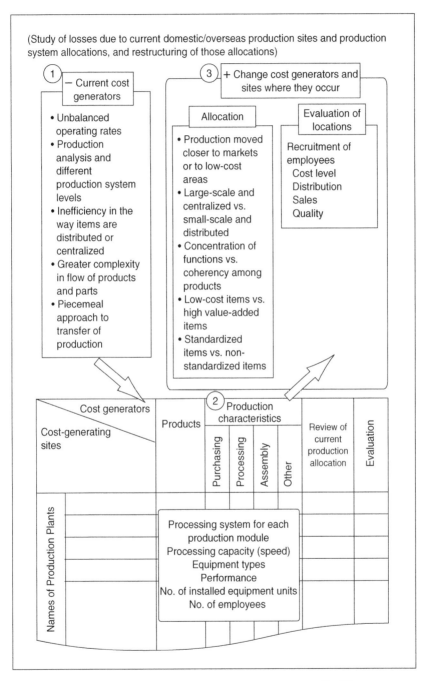

Figure 6-6. Techniques for Changes in Structures: ② Production Site/Changes in Production Allocation Structure

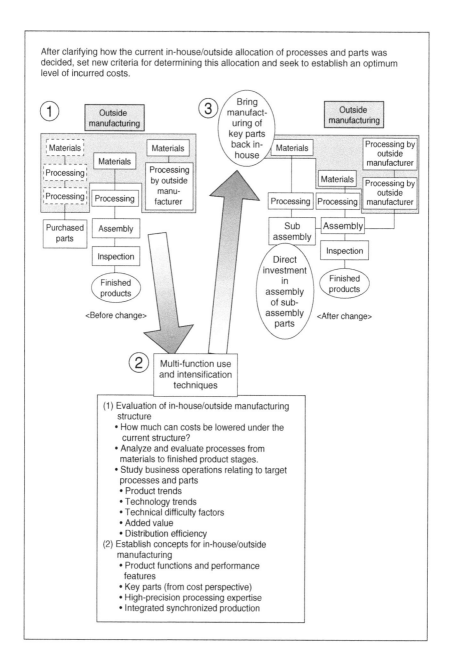

After clarifying how the current in-house/outside allocation of processes and parts was decided, set new criteria for determining this allocation and seek to establish an optimum level of incurred costs.

Figure 6-7. Techniques for Changes in Structures: ③ Change in Structure of In-House/Outside Manufacturing

main production line to intensify distribution processes. This case study involves a rather large number of parts and units. One of the key characteristics of the changes made by this company is that they applied multifunction use and intensification techniques at virtually every stage, from materials distribution to product assembly.

Changes in Materials and Purchasing Structures

How do you overcome the barriers to reducing purchasing-related costs? Ordinarily, among companies that produce popular consumer products, such as household electronics products or parts for such goods, the cost of materials (raw materials and parts) purchased from outside vendors accounts for 60 to 80 percent of the total manufacturing costs. This range is from 40 to 60 percent among companies that design and manufacture goods for other companies. Given these high percentages of costs for purchased goods, it is not a surprise that purchasing structures are a prime target for Cost Half activities.

No matter what the range of costs incurred by purchasing activities, companies such as those just depicted have carried out activities to reduce these costs in many ways, including the following:

1. Reviewing purchase specifications for precision, quality, and other standards.
2. Reviewing order parameters such as volumes, delivery periods, etc.
3. Changing vendors.
4. Requesting discounts when setting costs of purchased goods.
5. Providing assistance to make cost-saving improvements in vendors' manufacturing processes, especially outside vendors.

Such efforts have enabled these companies to reduce their purchased goods costs from 3 to 5 percent; however, they do nothing to change the purchasing structure as a whole. Nevertheless, you can make some degree of improvement in proportion to the amount of effort expended in these activities.

To achieve more, you must re-examine the entire purchasing structure and make some sweeping changes. The combination of a careful study of the purchasing structure and effective cost-cutting activities for purchased goods is a "double whammy" that will break down the barriers to substantial cost reductions.

Successful Cost-cutting Activities at EuZus Inc.   Let us briefly revisit EuZus Inc., whose cost reduction efforts were described in Chapter 1. Their efforts brought about a 43 percent cost savings, based on totals accumulated over half a business year. These results for ordered goods affected production output levels for 24 units over just half a year—quite an achievement.

EuZus Inc. focused on two objectives: 1) reducing the types and number of parts and 2) reducing the number of suppliers. Obviously, reducing the number of purchased parts will help reduce total costs for purchased goods. At the same time, each part that is no longer purchased from a supplier means less dependence on outside suppliers, which helps the company achieve objective 2. Moreover, the fewer suppliers utilized the less spent on costs related to management of outside purchases.

However, in the case of EuZus Inc., simply reducing the number of purchased parts was not enough to reduce the number of suppliers. EuZus had to make a conscious effort to explicitly shrink its pool of suppliers. Their efforts in this regard earned them another purchased goods cost cut-this time about 15 percent—which they accomplished by making the most of what they had learned after carefully re-evaluating their purchasing structure.

THE DRIVING FORCE FOR SHARING RECEIVED COSTS

There are seven steps in the re-evaluation of the purchasing structure, as illustrated in Figure 6-8.

First, and very importantly, you must check on the acceptable costs. After all, the review of the purchasing structure requires more than soliciting and reviewing ideas from the persons involved. It means a thorough review of supplier relationships, which often requires upper management decision-making. It also requires a purchasing review from the perspective of product design. Such reviews typically identify the need for design improvements in both products and parts. To make such improvements promptly and reliably, it is important to enlist the cooperation of personnel in the relevant departments.

Hold Discussions Based on Factual Data

It is very helpful to gather and analyze cost trend data before discussing possible courses of action. These discussions can help you cultivate the belief that purchasing costs must be determined using acceptable costs. There are two routes that you can take to propel your review of the purchasing structure. One route is a *re-*

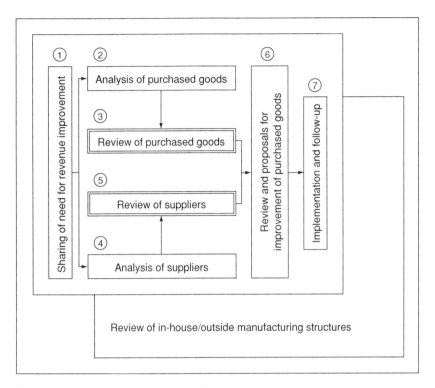

Figure 6-8. Techniques for Changes in Structures: ④ Steps in Re-evaluating the Materials Purchase Structure

view of purchased goods, which is step three in Figure 6-8, whereby you seek ways to improve the selection of purchased materials and parts. The other route is to *review the suppliers* (step five in Figure 6-8), which entails a re-evaluation of how suppliers have been selected, where they are located, and the suitability of the terms of the supply contract. The end result of these two endeavors is an encompassing review of your purchasing structure.

Route One: Review of Purchased Goods

Step three in Figure 6-8 is the analysis and review of purchased goods. There are three categories of purchased goods to consider: 1) materials, 2) finished parts, and 3) parts processed by an outside manufacturer. Refer to the purchased goods analysis shown in Figure 6-9. In this graph, the vertical axis represents the average unit

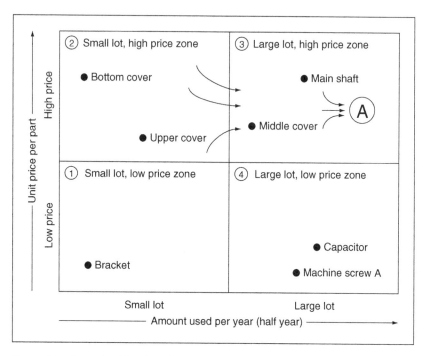

Figure 6-9. Analysis of Purchased Goods as Part of Review of Purchased Goods

price per part. The horizontal axis represents the number of parts used (purchased) per year or half year. Different types of parts are then plotted along these axes in an area that is divided into four zones, or quadrants. Making a graph such as this is quite a task for a company that manufactures a large assortment of products using a wide variety and large number of parts. The graph helps you pose the question, "Why must our company use such a wide variety and quantity of parts and materials?" Indeed, this is a very important question to bear in mind.

The Four Zones of Purchased Goods.   Once you draw the graph's two axes, divide the graph into the four zones entitled 1) small lot, low price zone, 2) small lot, high price zone, 3) large lot, high price zone, and 4) large lot, low price zone. Now you are ready to launch a review of purchased goods that are positioned in each of these four zones.

1. *Purchased goods in the small lot, low price zone.* These parts and materials are not often used in products but they are inexpensive,

so there is little value in purchasing them from outside suppliers. Instead, you should view the presence of such parts and materials as a shortcoming in the design of the products in which they are used. In other words, you should seek to correct this problem from the design perspective. The "bracket" referred to in the figure is one such part.

2. *Purchased goods in the small lot, high price zone.* You should place in this zone all the important parts that are needed to appeal to customers, particularly those that are distinctive in terms of their design or technology. In the graph, the "bottom cover" and "top cover" are examples of these kinds of parts. With regard to these two items, one should investigate whether they can be designed as common parts without detracting from their design or technology-related value. Making them common parts would reduce their cost as purchased goods. For important parts such as these, the concern should focus on their individual value. You should also consider whether it would be better to manufacture these parts in-house.

3. *Purchased goods in the large lot, high price zone.* This zone is very important in relation to costs. Consequently, parts and materials in this zone should be thoroughly studied as possible targets for standardization, simplification, and/or quantity reduction. If you can manufacture several of these parts using similar technology, you should also consider whether they should be manufactured in-house. Finally, check out whether you can purchase these same parts less expensively from other sources. In other words, you should try to move parts that appear in this zone as close as possible to the large lot, low price zone.

4. *Purchased goods in the large lot, low price zone.* Although items in this zone do not constitute an especially large share of the cost of purchased goods, you should not overlook them because they do involve substantial in-house costs, including assembly and procurement management costs. In its ongoing effort to discontinue using its own unique parts, the company should use, whenever possible, standard parts which are widely available in other markets. It is also out of the question for the company to subcontract production to outside manufacturers based on the company's own specifications. Using a method such as categorizing by series or arranging into groups helps standardize a wide variety of parts.

In summation, a re-evaluation of purchased goods means *changing the nature* of purchased goods. Reducing the number of purchased goods is but the first step in this re-evaluation of the purchasing structure.

A Preliminary Study Before Analyzing Purchased Goods. In some cases, you will need to make a preliminary study to determine whether you can analyze purchased goods in the manner depicted in Figure 6-9. At some companies, a very wide range of unit prices exists among parts that appear to serve similar functions. Before calculating an average price, the company should implement activities to narrow this range of unit prices. Typically, design factors have much to do with such wide-ranging variation in unit prices. However, some of this variation cannot be explained in terms of the materials used or differences in processing. In such cases, the variation is due to different levels of production output, or differences in the allocation of fixed costs or changeover costs. In many cases, companies launch development projects without first implementing a review of how unit prices are determined, and therefore end up maintaining unnecessarily high unit prices. By identifying and eliminating the factors behind high unit prices early on, companies can position their average unit costs at a more advantageous point in the graph shown in Figure 6-9. It is a good idea to create graphs such as this one for the various exterior parts, so you can categorize them as electrical equipment parts, machine parts, molding parts, and so on.

Route Two: Review of Suppliers

Step five in Figure 6-8 is the review of suppliers. The first step is to review suppliers' locations. The second step is to review the suppliers (vendors) themselves. You can categorize suppliers by the types of goods that they supply, such as sheet metal products, plastic-molded products, electronic devices, wiring parts, and so on, which helps also to set up a classification based on different production technologies. Whether the supplied goods are parts that have been processed by an outside manufacturer or other types of parts, what you are purchasing from these suppliers is their specialized technologies. Consequently, categorizing their supplied goods based on production technologies or product characteristics is an expedient means of conducting a thorough review.

When you study suppliers in terms of supplied goods that have been grouped in this manner, you can learn a lot about them. You should also remember that the more suppliers you use, the higher your procurement management costs will be. An overabundance of suppliers also makes it easier for you to overlook unnecessarily high unit prices for supplied goods. Unit prices tend to be especially high among the suppliers with whom you deal least often. Also, some supplier relationships may be based on formal or superficial reasons, and therefore not very beneficial from a purchasing standpoint.

The Four Zones of Suppliers.   Figure 6-10 shows another quadrant graph, this time for analyzing the range of suppliers. Here, the vertical axis represents the average (value-based) amount of orders per supplier per business year or half year.

The graph's horizontal axis represents the number of suppliers, or vendors. The "x" marks plotted in the graph represent suppliers that have been grouped according to categories of supplied goods, such as plastic molded parts and electronic devices. So we can see, for example, that $91,000 worth of plastic molded products were supplied by 15 different suppliers during the one-year period covered by the graph. It would be a good idea to break down the plastic molded parts further into categories of large and small parts. In this graph, each axis has been split in two to yield four quadrants: 1) small supplier base, low order level zone, 2) small supplier base, high order

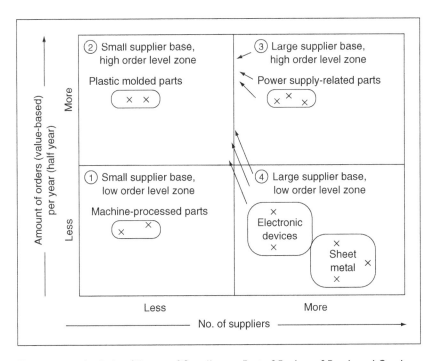

Figure 6-10. Analysis of Range of Suppliers as Part of Review of Purchased Goods

level zone, 3) large supplier base, high order level zone, and 4) large supplier base, low order level zone. Our review of suppliers will cover each of these zones separately

1. *Small supplier base, low order level zone.* This zone represents low-value transactions. We should try to reduce the number of these transactions; for instance, by changing suppliers. Any transaction made in this zone should be considered a factor in contributing to unnecessarily high costs. EuZus Inc.'s transactions with suppliers of machine-processed parts fall into this zone. EuZus Inc. was able to shift these transactions to another supplier by changing product designs so that they could use sheet metal parts instead of machine-processed parts.

2. *Small supplier base, high order level zone.* Basically, in this zone transactions tend to be advantageous. Because the suppliers in this zone supply large amounts of ordered goods, this is an area in which you can effectively reduce costs by devising and implementing improvements in specifications for purchased goods or in ordering-related conditions.

3. *Large supplier base, high order level zone.* The majority of purchasing costs resides in this zone. Here, it is important to find ways to move items in this zone toward the "A" position in the graph. In other words, you should try to establish more favorable purchasing conditions among your suppliers, such as concentrating your transactions with just a few of them. As you study these possibilities, seek to establish an optimum level of transactions with an optimum number of suppliers.

4. *Large supplier base, low order level zone.* This zone represents purchasing activities involving a large number of suppliers combined with a relatively small amount of orders. Although you should avoid this zone, it is important to understand how transactions within it came to be established. Was it because of a tendency to find new suppliers for each newly developed product? Or because the person in charge selects suppliers based simply on scheduling? Studies tend to reveal that factors such as these are often the cause of unprofitable purchasing activities in this zone. After identifying and eliminating such factors, you can study ways to reduce the number of these suppliers and shift these transactions toward a high-order level zone.

The Importance of Switching to the Most Advantageous Suppliers. The basic point of the foregoing discussion is that you must identify and re-evaluate suppliers who impose conditions that prevent advantageous purchasing. This includes suppliers that are added on just because a new product has been developed, suppliers that are selected based primarily on scheduling considerations, and groups of suppliers that increase in number because you need a rapid boost in production output. You should then establish conditions that encourage suppliers to work harder to achieve lower costs, faster delivery, and higher quality. After all, there is no use in asking for more extensive cooperation from suppliers unless the suppliers themselves are first motivated, and the major condition that motivates them is the number of orders they stand to receive. You must come to realize that, even in cases where it appears to be cheaper to deal with a variety of suppliers who will submit various bids to compare, on a total cost basis this approach is not necessarily cheaper.

Clarify the Roles Played by Various Departments

Implementing measures are based on two kinds of reviews of the purchasing structure: one directed at purchased goods and the other at the companies that supply those goods. We might sum up these reviews as an approach that asks, "Which parts should we order from which suppliers, and how can we make the changes needed to do that?" After conducting reviews to answer the first part of that question, you are ready to address the second part, using the information on suppliers and parts from those reviews. At this juncture, it is time to consider the roles played by various departments, such as the design department, the materials procurement department, and even upper management. Last but not least, it is also important to involve the suppliers themselves in the implementation phase. The best way to launch this phase is to put together a project team.

Summary of the Changes in Purchasing Structure

Figure 6-11 sums up the changes in purchasing structure that have been described in this chapter. For a further recap, see the seven steps in the re-evaluation of the purchasing structure, as illustrated in Figure 6-8.

The summary in Figure 6-11 has three main parts:

1. You clarify the characteristics of the current purchasing structure. When doing this, notice which suppliers you use simply out of

Purpose: To take a fresh look at the purchasing structure, which has been shaped by the company's history, its past responses to problems, etc., with a view toward optimizing incurred costs.

①

Current purchasing structure

- Regular suppliers, determined largely by habit
- Range of suppliers and purchased goods, which has increased in tandem with new product development

③

Review of purchasing structure

- Key functions: Development by other company, joint development with other company, in-house design with outsourced production
- Prerequisites for selection of suppliers: status as in/not in traditional group of affiliated companies
- Area of supplier candidates: overseas/domestic
- Ordering system: Centralized ordering/decentralized ordering
- Bidding system: Competitive bidding/price controlled by our company
- Contract system: Implied contract, negotiated each time/based on annual unit cost trends/based on processing points/based on maintaining scheduled unit prices

②   Analysis of purchased goods

Analysis of suppliers	Name of part	Supplier	Value of order	Quantity of order	Part characteristics

Supplier	Part	Annual order amount	Function of supplier			
			Technical development	Design	Production	Distribution
A	a		○	○	○	○
	b			○	○	○
	c			○	○	○
B	d				○	○
	e				○	○
	f				○	○

Figure 6-11. Summary of Changes in Purchasing Structure

habit, as well as other habitual behaviors. In this way you can identify the characteristics of purchasing methods that are tied to product development.

2. You analyze purchased goods and their suppliers as well as the systems described in part 3. You can use the table shown in this part of the figure to collect data.

3. You use these considerations to provide clues as to the best direction for changing the purchasing structure. Factors to be considered include the functions that your company depends on suppliers to fulfill, prerequisites for selecting suppliers, domestic/overseas locations of candidate suppliers, and the ordering, bidding, and contract systems.

Now we will move on to Chapter 7 to discuss the last three Cost Half techniques: changes in logic, process changes, and activity changes.

Cost Half Techniques 3 through 5: Changes in Logic, Process Changes, and Activity Changes

As mentioned in Chapter 4, the five Cost Half techniques are *the instruments of change* in the Cost Half program. Some of these techniques focus on reducing item costs; others focus on reducing process costs. To refresh your memory, Figure 4-3 reviews the way the five techniques interface with item costs and processes.

COST HALF TECHNIQUE 3: CHANGES IN LOGIC

Changes in logic represent one of the Cost Half techniques for reducing item costs. As was described in Figure 4-8, when preconditions and limitations exist, you can start exploring new ideas by eliminating them. By comparison, changes in logic extend deeply into the conceptual design process as a means of launching new ideas.

Refer to Figure 7-1. This flowchart showing logic change techniques happens to concern seals used in products such as automobiles. The designs for these seals must meet various requirements. In this case, the seals must have high-level soundproofing and moisture-proofing characteristics. Three design elements should be considered in order to meet these requirements.

The first design element is surface pressure. A certain amount of pressure must exist to maintain the seal's contact with the target surface. Any gap between the seal and the target surface creates problems for maintaining the required hermetic seal.

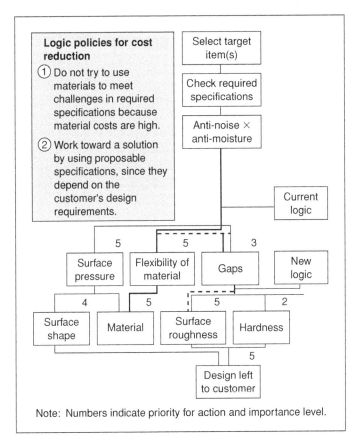

Figure 7-1. Techniques for Changes in Logic

The cost breakdown for these seals is 90 percent for materials and 10 percent for processing. Therefore, the material cost must be lowered in order to make any substantial reduction in the seals' total cost. Consequently, it is a good idea to select the logic of focusing on the gap size, since that has little to do with material costs. The numbers that appear next to the boxes in the flowchart in Figure 7-1 indicate the amount of attention paid to a particular element. Higher numbers (more points) indicate more attention. In this example, the gap issue is given only three points, which indicates only an average amount of attention from designers. Giving more attention to this issue would mean a change in logic. Naturally, since these seals will be used in products (such as automobiles) that are being developed based on customers' demands, any such change in logic must be coordinated with those customers' own design ideas. In this case, the result was that the company devised a new way of using the material, which enabled them to cut costs.

Choosing the Appropriate Design-Activity Path

Design activities follow certain paths, and typically you can take many different paths to meet the specified requirements. Obviously, it's important to choose the appropriate design-activity path, since the cost differences incurred by the various paths can be great indeed.

The analysis of changing the logic is summarized below.

1. Establish cost-cutting policies.
2. Select target items whose costs are to be lowered by logic changes.
3. Clarify the required specifications, then start asking designers to consider what is needed to meet those specifications.
4. Check at each stage for logical alternative ideas.
5. If such alternatives are found, have the designers consider them.

Draw up a chart that graphs both the existing logic and the proposed logic. Now you are ready to clarify the current logic route and start experimenting with proposed logic changes. Sometimes you can hatch great new ideas simply by trying out a different logic combination. The ultimate goal is to find the optimum logic route for achieving both the design objective and the target cost, after which you will still need to elucidate further the technical issues. Through experimentation and discussion, you can pinpoint all of the remaining unknown factors.

When defining the technical issues, important points to consider typically include not only those the product design staff needs to analyze but also various issues that the production engineering department and other departments must investigate. The logic of design concepts depends on the experience and perspective of each designer: a positive outcome from the design concept is referred to as "original"; a negative outcome is called "egocentric." When it comes to costs, though, neither originality nor egocentricity matter much—what does matter are the plain facts. Consequently, the important point is that logic changes should be based on an understanding and factual analysis of cost generators.

COST HALF TECHNIQUE 4: PROCESS CHANGES

Since many companies have some experience in the use of concurrent engineering consulting to promote process changes (PC for short) as a key process innovation approach, let us make concurrent engineering our starting point.

When concerned with the product development process, for example, the product development staff applies PC to all the processes spanning early development stages to the disposal stage for old products. (The product development staff includes not only the product designers but also the production engineers and staff in the materials purchasing, quality assurance, sales, and distribution departments.) This is done to clarify the quality, cost, and delivery (QCD) objectives at each of these stages. Other objectives achievable through this approach include shortened development lead time and reduced labor requirements.

There are three principles of PC:

1. *Parallel processing.* As is suggested by the etymology of the word concurrent (con = "with" and current = "flow of time") in the phrase "concurrent engineering," you can make progress in several improvements simultaneously through parallel processing.
2. *Source processing.* Make latent problems apparent as early on as possible, so as to derive maximum benefit from problem-solving efforts as a function of source processing. This is a very effective way to minimize wasteful back-tracking and reworking that can occur at later development stages due to belatedly discovered problems.
3. *Coordination processing.* The coordination processing work that the project manager performs to spur progress toward the objectives.

Figure 7-2 charts these three principles of PC.

To change your processes, you must view the links among tasks as processes. Figure 7-3 provides an example.

Review Current Processes–Five Patterns that Increase Cost Generators

Why have the processes used so far failed to shorten lead time, and why have cost generators been increasing? The following five patterns have repeatedly emerged in case studies.

1. *Project planning functions are weak.* A familiar pattern in which progress is made due mainly to deadline pressure, not planning; this usually means your process planning is inadequate.

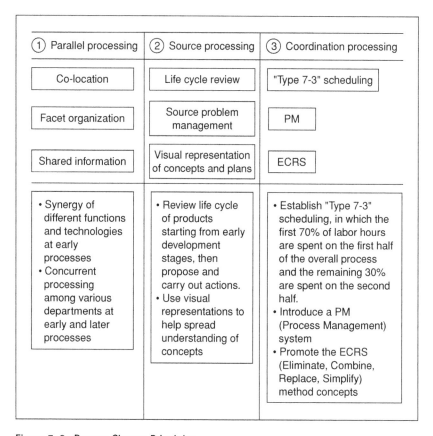

Figure 7–2. Process Change Principles

2. *Have not established early management system or methods to eval-uate the completeness of quality and cost planning.* A pattern in which problems are dealt with only as they arise, without sufficient planning to anticipate or prevent them.

3. *Poor ability to grasp and communicate concepts and ideas.* A pattern whereby people go about their work with neither a sense of direction nor clear goals. Sometimes, the direction of work changes later on and work must be redone.

4. *Inadequate sharing of information.* Are people informed as to who is doing what? All too often, the routine dictates that people simply apply their own interpretation of how their tasks should be performed. They are not well informed about what others are doing. This leads to duplication of effort and rework.

5. *Knowledge is not being circulated and re-utilized, so projects are not being reviewed thoroughly.* In this pattern, mistakes are end-

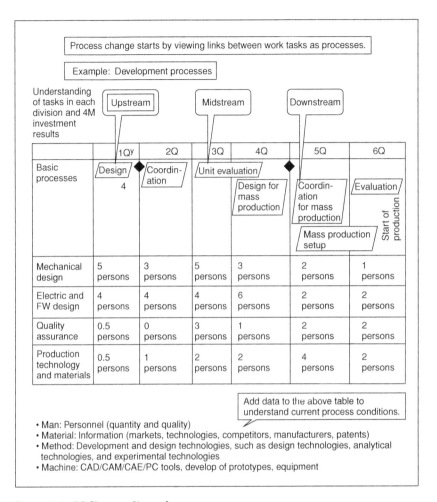

Figure 7–3. PC (Process Change)

lessly repeated; there is no steady accumulation of knowledge, so people do not learn from each others' experiences.

SIX PC MEASURES TO BREAK COST-GENERATING PATTERNS

Undoubtedly, you can find examples similar to the patterns described above all around you. After reflecting on these patterns, any type of company can successfully implement PC—which is to say, shorter lead time and more efficient and effective work processes—by carrying out the six measures we will next discuss in this section.

Since processes related to product development comprise the largest group of processes at most manufacturing companies, these six PC measures are based on those processes.

Measure 1: Design and Management of 7–3 Type Processes

Figure 7-4 presents a division/development stage breakdown of how development labor hours are traditionally analyzed. The broken line in the graph to the right of the schedule table clearly depicts that de-

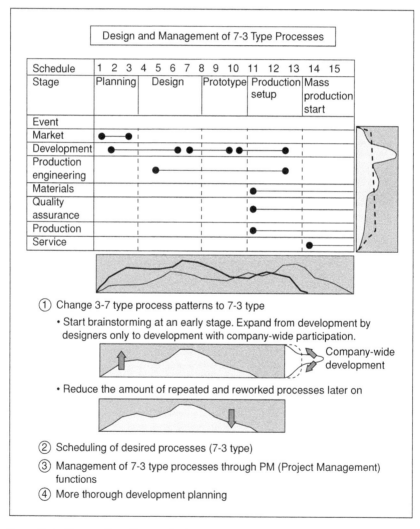

Figure 7-4. The 7-3 Type Process Design

signers dominate development tasks— involvement by other divisions is much less. The thin solid line in the graph below the schedule table shows that only about 30 percent of the labor hours occur before the halfway point; the other 70 percent occur during the second half, as deadline pressures build. This is an example of 3-7 type processes.

Consequently, it is important to redesign processes so that the pattern can be reversed—from 3-7 type processes to 7-3 type processes (see item ① in Figure 7-4). First, you can break the practice of letting designers dominate the planning process by opening some of the early management brainstorming work to employees throughout the company. Together, they can devise ways to avoid repeated and reworked processes that have been occurring downstream (second half), thereby moving a greater share of labor hours upstream (first half). Three steps toward accomplishing this are listed in Figure 7-4 as ② scheduling (and 5H analysis) of desired processes (7-3 type), ③ stronger management of processes through project management functions, and ④ more thorough development planning to produce more meaningful and complete schedules. It is important to implement these steps before you launch the development project. When all four items in Figure 7-4—① ② ③ ④—are successfully implemented, development lead time will begin to shrink.

Measure 2: Management of Early Problems and Exploration of Hypothetical Issues

The concurrent engineering approach calls for many people who are knowledgeable in various areas to work concurrently on a wide range of activities. In such situations, it is vital that project members ask themselves what they can do, and when, to assist this team effort. However, starting from an early stage of development, project members must share a roadmap of the means planned to achieve the product development goals. Lacking such guidance, members will find it harder to understand what to do next or how important their activities truly are to the entire project. This has led to situations where progress among project members has come to a halt.

To help establish a roadmap of project activities, start by identifying (i.e., making apparent) issues that can occur at each phase of the early conceptual planning stage. Next, allow members to brainstorm for solutions to these issues, and start planning a set of development processes that address each of them. The team members then share this information with all concerned, so that everyone is better prepared when the development project reaches the starting block.

Typically, product information for users (such as that contained in owner's manuals and catalogues) is produced *after* the product in question has been made. But such information could also be used at early development stages to help project members gain a clearer image of what it is they are developing. (The information included in a product manual or catalogue would be somewhat different, of course.)

Figure 7-5 is a concept development diagram that is intended to provide an opportunity to clarify concepts and determine which issues need to be addressed early on. In other words, it provides a framework for listing concerns that have not yet been listed or specifications that have not yet appeared in the catalogue.

At first, it may seem like a lot of trouble to create a development diagram and attempt to anticipate various issues. But this is actually a very effective tool that yields big returns on the time invested, because it eliminates backtracking steps at later stages.

Measure 3: Proactive Management

The next measure is managing proactively, in a way that anticipates problems. The typical approach at many companies is simply to deal with problems as they arise. When managers take this latter approach, they can never say for sure how far along the project is or how much remains to be done.

Companies that have acquired ISO-9000 certification possess materials that they probably have barely touched since they were certified, such as various rules and standards for tasks (design review, quality review, etc.) at each production stage. These materials need to be reconsidered and reapplied for the same processes *as they currently exist*.

Control checkpoints (usually in the form of reviews by audit committees such as the conceptual planning review committee, commercial planning review committee, and mass production transfer review committee) should be placed where employees can ask questions such as: What are our goals? What hurdles must we clear to succeed? What are our evaluation standards and methods? Who should be included in these efforts? Placing questions such as these on cards and distributing them to relevant staff at certain stages of the development schedule helps provide a basis for better progress management.

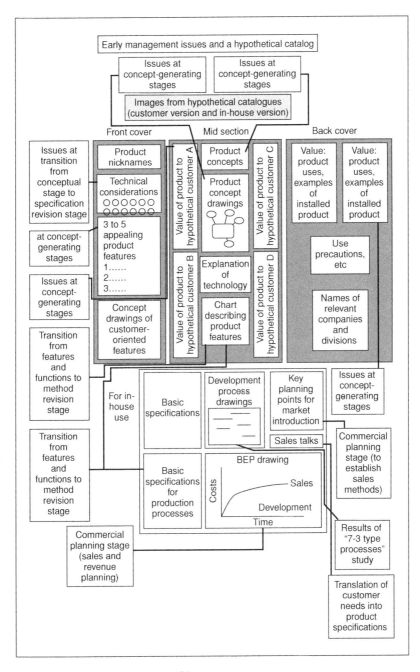

Figure 7-5. Concept Development Diagram

If a project fails to clear certain hurdles at certain control points (i.e., reviews), it is time to work on the project until it *can* clear those hurdles. This ensures that the project will not go forward regardless of shortcomings—which would inevitably result in having to back-track at some later stage, in a sort of "saw-blade" pattern of a few steps forward followed by a step or two backward. Instead, the project will move steadily onward and upward from stage to stage, like a stairway.

Although many companies have won total quality control (TQC) awards or ISO certification by establishing detailed rules and regulations, it is ironic that so few of those rules and regulations are applicable for managing actual processes. Many companies exhibit a long-ingrained habit of going through the same old motions at the review stages, passing along projects that do not pass all of the checkpoints and assuming that problems will be fixed "later." Sometimes, project team members go to the extra trouble of making several types of parts or materials available to use as alternatives, on the assumption that they may be needed if problems arise later on. When they do this, they think they are being good "team players" and are helping the project, when in fact they are generally harming it.

Measure 4: Actions to Establish Higher Control Standards for Problems

Returning to the topic of progress management through the various development stages, let's consider the importance of understanding the issues involved in progress management.

Let's say that when you are developing a certain product you receive one point in what we shall term *problem management value* for every issue you resolve during the development process. Furthermore, you can multiply this value by a percentage score (we'll call it the *comprehension rate*) that indicates the degree to which each issue has been understood. You can multiply this again by another percentage score (let's call this the *problem response score*) that indicates whether or not each issue has been met with a response action.

For example, if there are 100 issues but only 50 of them have been recognized and understood, and if only half of those have been met with a response action, then the resulting problem management value would be 25 points, or 25 percent of a possible total of 100 percent in problem management value.

Thus, it is important to establish early on how many issues exist. If the manager figures that there are only 50 issues when there are actually 100, and manages to resolve 25 of them, then that manager will mistakenly assume that only another 25 issues remain to be resolved. In such a case, the hitherto unrecognized 50 issues *will* become apparent later on—for instance, when tooling up for mass production—and the manager will end up working day and night to deal with them.

In other words, if our understanding of problems and issues at an early stage is inadequate, we can be sure that additional problems will surface at downstream processes. Since you cannot deal with problems until they are recognized as being such, it is hard to overstate the need for project members to work hard at an early stage to identify problems.

Measure 5: Organization and Location for Information-Sharing to Support Necessary Functions

The four measures described so far are all oriented toward successful process changes. Measure 5 is concerned with the question of building a process execution system. Since processes constitute the lifeblood of production, the execution system you establish to perform them is very important indeed.

An organization is like a cut diamond in that if one facet is clouded, the other facets will also be clouded. One of these facets is the system or method used to select project members. You must choose members carefully, matching particular skills with specific functions. If you select project team members based solely on some vague notion that so-and-so would be good at this or that, you will end up with members who are actually ill-suited for their assignments, with assignments that are redundant, and/or with members who have been selected primarily because they know one another and get along well.

Instead, you should recruit project team members in the same manner in which soldiers are recruited for war: by making sure all essential functions are covered without unnecessary duplication of effort and by strengthening "battle formations" to avoid "front-line losses."

Many companies that have implemented this approach have discovered an environment in which they gain synergistic effects by keeping various development project members and their workplaces in close touch, either via physical proximity or through close electronic communications such as e-mail. When members of different projects work close to one another, they can more easily learn about the results of each other's efforts, the concepts they have used, and the problems they have discovered. Such communication is very meaningful in many ways. However, it takes major motivation and effort to get this information across to people through face-to-face contact.

To help share such information among various project members, the company should set up a "virtual-environment" database for project-related information on its in-house network. The company should also set up a "project room"—a physical location where members can gather to discuss their projects first-hand, often with remarkably beneficial results.

Measure 6: Fired-up Motivation and Knowledge Management

For any game or contest to be worthwhile, those participating must be motivated to play hard. Accordingly, getting people motivating staff is an essential measure for development projects. Project members should be motivated at every opportunity; i.e., receiving some kind of recognition when each development stage is completed, with special recognition for reaching each important stage or threshold. Some companies hold meetings to bestow awards, such as "MVP" awards for the most successful or hard-working project members.

Managerial tasks for development projects have hitherto rolled along on two axes—one being *process management,* which manages the progress being made at each process or step in each development stage, and the other being *document management,* which manages the various documents produced and used for development projects. The Cost Half approach adds a third axis to this, called *knowledge management.* This is where you store, update, and share the collective knowledge of veteran project members.

Just as individuals enjoy discovering new things and increasing their own knowledge, companies also have much to gain by nurturing and effectively utilizing the collective knowledge of their employees. In recent years, this has become an increasingly vital corporate asset, and thus an important management theme.

THE FIRST STEP IN PC: A LOOK BACKWARD TO RECENT DEVELOPMENT PROJECTS

Having just described six measures that will help ensure successful process changes, let us now turn to the question of how to proceed. Our first step should be to take a look backward. As demonstrated in

Figure 7-4, in order to understand what kinds of development efforts have been made to date it helps to analyze any recent development projects that you have implemented for similar products. You should check the documentation to find out what had been planned at the beginning of those projects, and what kind of results were achieved. Apply Post-it® notes to descriptions of efforts that failed to go as planned, and record where and when problems arose. Later, you can categorize the problems as *technical issues, work process issues,* or *management issues.* Finally, you should look for any measures that were devised to address the problems and attach Post-it® notes to the relevant documents. Ordinarily, this work takes about three days. Ideas tend to come together on the second day, so groups often split these activities into a two-day session followed later by a one-day session.

Using the insights gained from these exercises, project members are now ready to start planning the development processes for the next project. Besides establishing processes as 7-3 type processes in terms of distribution of labor hours, they must restructure their approach and include additional strategic elements, such as deploying new managerial or operational concepts, new technology development policies, and new marketing measures.

Strengthening the Development Organization

To make these processes even stronger, members should employ the *series development concept,* which considers not only the development of individual products but also other production-related factors such as how production equipment is being utilized. They also should focus on setting up *element technology development* to enable more accurate responses to new product needs, while gearing up for new technologies and establishing a pipeline to markets by facilitating the gathering and communication of input from customers concerning their needs and wants. Thus, process changes involve more than shortening lead times and cutting costs: they start and end with activities that help build stronger processes.

COST HALF TECHNIQUE 5: ACTIVITY CHANGES

After changing processes, it remains to change behavior (i.e., activities). You can eliminate many cost generators simply by changing the way people do their work. From any point of view, there is much to be gained by improving activities.

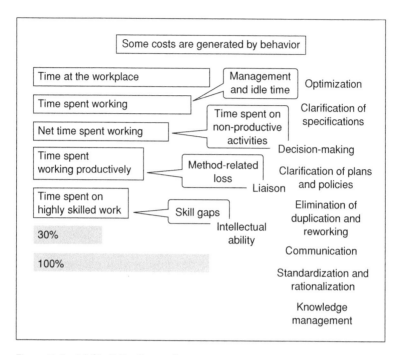

Figure 7-6. AC (Activity Changes)

Figure 7-6 shows results from a work sampling study done in a certain company's development and design divisions. By breaking work down according to degrees of quality (as productive work), you can see that highly skilled, productive work comprises only about 30 percent of the time that employees spend at the workplace. The work done in product development processes, for example, shows that the content of the work differs at different development stages (early stage, production start stage, etc.). However, such stage-related differences do not make much difference in the amount of time spent on highly skilled work as a percentage of the total time at the workplace. As Figure 7-6 illustrates, many factors stand in the way of improving the productivity of time spent at the workplace: management and idle time, time spent on nonproductive activities, loss due to nonproductive methods, and loss due to skill gaps. The root problem is not so much the nonproductive activities themselves as it is the environment that supports such activities.

Figures 7-7 and 7-8 show examples of activity changes (AC) that differ according to the stage of activities. In Figure 7-7 activities were studied at the design stage, and the figure shows that much

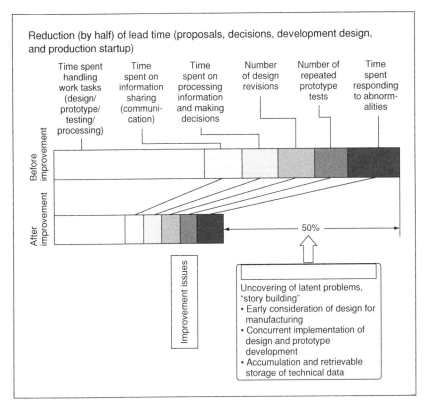

Figure 7-7. AC (Example) ①

time was being spent on responding to abnormalities, making design revisions, and sharing information. Often in these cases people were checking or clarifying work done at an upstream process. Figure 7-7 also shows that implementing the Cost Half approach was indeed effective in reducing lead time and its associated labor costs.

The other example in Figure 7-8 also concerns the design stage, but in this case more measurements were taken at early processes. Therefore, it is to be expected that considerable time was spent on conceptual design work, but there was also significant rework and duplicated work. Obviously, more proactive management is needed, along with a greater emphasis on developing hypotheses prior to implementation.

Many of the problems in this example involve time management. This company spent too much time in meetings and on the collection and reporting of data—as much as 30 percent of its labor hours. The

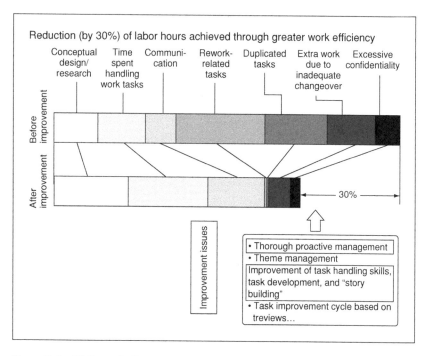

Figure 7–8. AC Example ②

higher-ups were clearly ordering their subordinates to spend excessive time writing reports and presenting data. This company needed to establish other, more efficient ways to gather and use information.

When scheduling is unclear or inadequate, you waste time on nonproductive work. This leads to a need for subsequent revisions to schedules, and it creates work that is directed toward the wrong goals, which also wastes time. In this case, there were also many problems with the progress management of work tasks. When people always do things in the same old habitual way, some work gets misdirected and must be redone.

Work Standardization and Knowledge Management

It is only natural that highly skilled people work better and faster than do those less-skilled. That is why a work standardization and knowledge management perspective is imperative when seeking out and eliminating cost generators. Your goal in implementing AC techniques should be to double the efficiency of work-related actions, for instance from 30 percent to 60 percent. While acknowledging that modes of behavior and attitudes are important aspects of work efficiency, employees at this company needed also to bear in mind the sobering fact that they were spending only about 30 percent of their labor hours engaged in activities directly related to achieving their goals.

As mentioned earlier in our discussion of the sixth PC measure for breaking cost-generating patterns, knowledge management is the third axis for managerial tasks relating to development projects (process management and document management being the other two). By collecting and sharing the knowledge of veteran project members, this company could have created a vital corporate asset and a management strategy that would have helped reduce the 70 percent of labor hours wasted on indirect activities unrelated to the achievement of its goals.

We are now ready to move on to Chapter 8, which describes at length each of the five steps used when introducing Cost Half activities:

- Design the target;
- Analyze cost generating sources and locations;
- Apply the five Cost Half techniques to propose actions and scenarios;
- Manage Cost Half measures and results; and
- Build and operate a Cost Half cost management system.

....

8

....

Cost Half Deployment

This chapter describes the five steps used when introducing Cost Half activities. In the course of these activities, it is important that everyone work toward a common goal and coordinate their efforts for maximum effect. To do so, a company must begin by clearly delineating the road that lies ahead. Therefore you should be very careful to ensure that, right from the first step, all participants gain and share a clear understanding of both goals and methodology.

Along with sharing the same goals, your company must share the pooled knowledge needed to achieve those goals, including knowledge of the methods to be used. Also, you must share the results of cost analysis, jointly devise Cost Half measures, jointly overcome obstacles to success, share the same vision of what is to be implemented, and implement management that crosses the boundaries of departmental and individual areas of responsibility. All of these practices improve the overall organization, and thereby extend Cost Half activities beyond the scope of the assigned tasks.

Of course, the methods you do use in these activities must be appropriate for achieving the two overarching goals of the Cost Half: 1) improving the company's bottom-line profitability, and 2) lowering product cost levels.

REVIEW OF COST HALF PROGRAM—THE FIVE STEPS

In Chapters 4 through 7, we presented a general introduction to the Cost Half program. Before describing the implementation of a Cost Half project, let's use Figure 8-1 for a quick review. This figure summarizes the contents of steps 1 to 5 (i.e., I to V) that we originally discussed in Chapter 3. The process cost team heading in the figure is where you enter the name of the particular Cost Half team. This process cost team sets process cost targets and implements activities to achieve them. Naturally, the item cost team is responsible for item costs while the process cost team is responsible for process costs. The cost management team is responsible for designing targets and building as well as managing a cost management system.

The time required for Cost Half activities includes about one month for the target design at Step 1, about two months for the analysis of cost-generating locations at Step 2, and about two or three months for proposing implementation measures and scenarios at Step 3. The amount of time needed to collect the results of implementing Cost Half measures at Step 4 depends on the scope of the company's Cost Half project. Generally, the results are achieved in about six months and are managed thereafter. You should hold a results management meeting regularly, such as on a monthly basis.

The building and management of a cost management system, which occurs concurrently with Step 4, takes about three to five months for the building phase. The operation phase, Step 5, follows. It is important to start the management phase in sync with the relevant product development timing, especially in the case of a new product.

These estimates of required time periods will vary depending on the activity types and targets. However, these estimates have proven typical in previous projects and therefore provide a general guideline.

Let us begin our step-by-step description of Cost Half activities, starting with Step 1.

Step 1: Design the Target

The key components of step 1 are as follows:

- Envision the type of business to be achieved
- Determine target cost levels
- Determine acceptable costs
- Allot acceptable costs

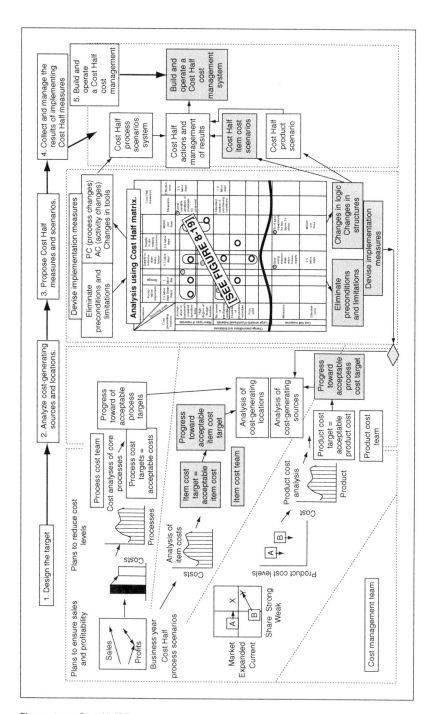

Figure 8-1. Cost Half Program

This step shows you how to break down and manage targets (goals) under the Cost Half approach. This kind of detailed breakdown of targets is intended to bring the results of Cost Half activities as close as possible to the envisioned improvement in business performance. It is also part of the Cost Half orientation toward building a stronger overall organization. As you accumulate more and more improvements that reduce costs, you can be sure that various forms of loss and waste will be eliminated. But to truly strengthen the overall organization, you must also apply your cost-cutting results to redirect your approach to specific products, processes, and systems.

Envision the Type of Business You Want to Become. At this step, the Cost Half team is asked to envision the kinds of results they wish to achieve over the next three to five years in the business operations targeted by their Cost Half activities. That is, they are to devise an image of Cost Half results or desired business results. Of course, positive results from Cost Half activities should also be expected in the current year and next year—not just three to five years ahead. Whatever the results, they must be tied to creating a stronger overall company organization or their significance as Cost Half activity results will be meager at best.

Accordingly, the Cost Half team should envision a new structure for the company, one that ties in with stronger profitability, which means planning to ensure higher sales and profits. This planning should include a vision of the company's future competitive products, that is, products that will be cost-competitive enough to attract buyers in target markets.

The deployed plans will include improvement plans for achieving target levels in basic costs and product costs. Naturally, the team will need to envision results for other types of improvements as well. For example, consider the plans for improving business functions, product development, and personnel downsizing, shown in Figure 8-2.

Let's first turn to operational planning. To begin planning to ensure sales and profits, start by envisioning the desired profit level. There are many factors to consider when setting an organization's sales-profit rate (pre-tax profit rate, expressed as a percentage).

The need for an improvement plan is especially clear in cases where the sales-profit rate has been declining, has stayed flat, or has been only modest compared to the sales-profit rates of competing companies. Even after target values have been set, you may need to hold meetings to help ensure attainment of the targets, such as meetings to analyze and review operations and cost structures.

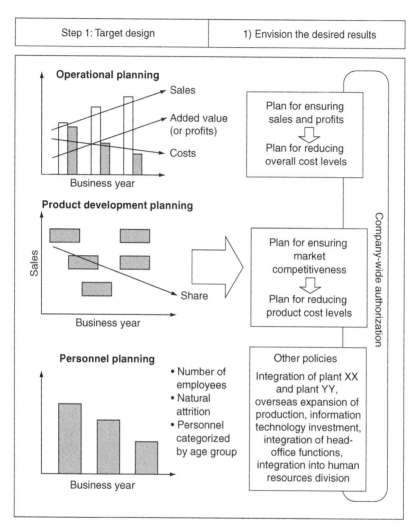

Figure 8-2. Improving Business Functions, Product Development, and Personnel Downsizing

Product development planning includes elucidation of a plan to ensure market competitiveness. This involves studying the requirements that planned new products will need to compete effectively in the marketplace. To establish a plan for reducing product cost levels, effective product pricing must be planned ahead for at least the next three years.

In some cases, you may need a merchandising strategy like the one in Figure 8-3 as part of this planning step. Propose measures for key products in response to market trends. In particular, the idea is to set sales prices that are market-competitive.

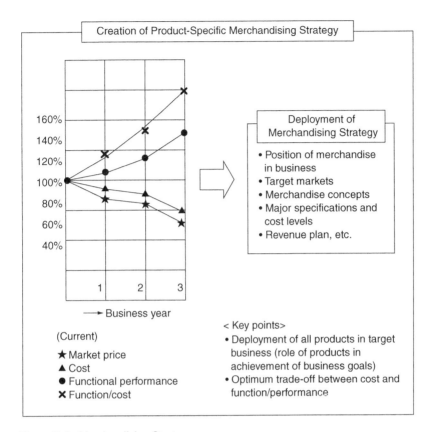

Figure 8-3. Merchandizing Strategy

You can easily estimate a product's marketable price by calculating the cost required to produce the functionality and performance characteristics needed for the target market. We can draw a curve similar to that of the marketable price by analyzing sales price trends for similar products. The function/cost ratio should not be based on the preconception that higher functionality necessarily means higher cost. Lower cost relative to higher functionality yields higher cost performance, as is shown in Figure 8-3.

As Figure 8-2 showed, the plan for ensuring sales and profits is based on an investigation of the entire enterprise. The plan for ensuring market competitiveness is based on an investigation of the main product groups. The Cost Half approach combines these two plans to pursue the ultimate goal, which is to build a stronger organization.

Determine the Target Cost Level.   Figure 8-4 illustrates how the target cost level for Cost Half activities is determined based on the

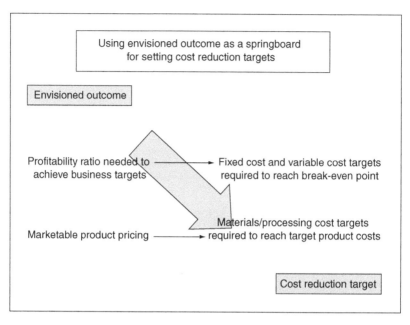

Figure 8-4. Determining the Target Cost Reduction Target

profitability ratio needed to achieve business targets, which in turn is based on marketable product pricing and the target sales price level.

Figure 8-5 illustrates how target cost levels are determined, which occurs at Step 1.

First, let us consider an example of how the overall cost level is determined (the overall cost is the total sales value minus the operating costs). In Figure 8-5, a value of 100 is assigned as the current sales total, and percentage share values are assigned to the various expense and revenue items. In this example, the operating profit is a mere 1.5 percent, which is not enough to meet the business target. To reach this target, you must raise the operating profit to 6 percent, which is still not a high value.

In some cases, an operating profit of about 10 percent would be a desirable minimum. As long as total sales stay flat, the only way to raise the profitability level is to reduce costs, such as manufacturing costs, as is shown in Figure 8-5.

Therefore, the first task is to determine whether you can find ways to lower not only manufacturing costs but also sales expenses and other general expenses. For reference's sake, you might find out what the cost configuration was previously when the company had

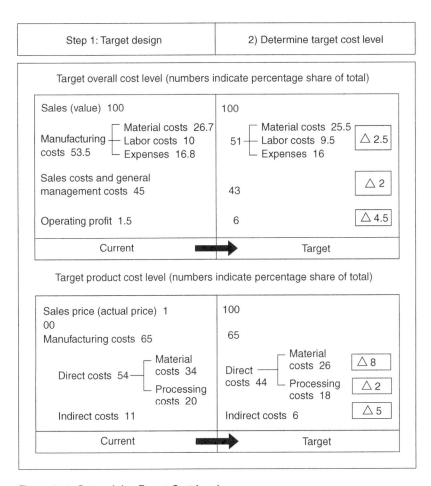

Figure 8-5. Determining Target Cost Levels

its best profitability situation, or you might check the cost configuration of competing companies. You must also pay attention to how quickly costs rise at your own company.

When sales expenses and general management expenses grow rapidly, the Cost Half teams should consider them areas that require scrutiny and discussion. In many cases, the teams have sought to reduce sales expenses and general management expenses relative to manufacturing costs. When determining the target product cost level, it is important to carefully consider the predominant sales price. When the selling price goes down due to competition, it suggests that products in certain manufacturing categories will be produced at a loss.

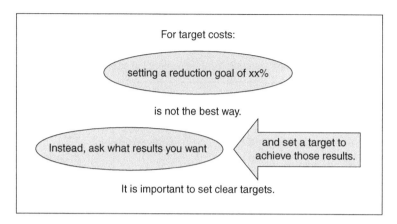

Figure 8-6. Tips About Setting Targets

Often, such problems are compounded by the fact that little can be done to change sales policies. The bottom part of Figure 8-5 shows the configuration of manufacturing costs and associated specific costs when you assign the sales price a value of 100.

After determining that the manufacturing costs must be about 50 points lower than the sales cost, the team decided the goal should be to reduce manufacturing costs that are specified as direct costs or indirect costs. In this case, too, they found problems when studying the relative shares of material costs, processing costs, and indirect costs. To move in the right direction toward answering the question of which costs deserve the most attention, the team should check the configuration that existed when profitability was highest and should identify the costs that have grown most rapidly. Since outsourcing expenses are included in material costs and processing costs, the percentage share of outsourcing expenses is significant and should be considered. If production yields are not on the rise and internal manufacturing capacity exists, there is no excuse for having a high share of outsourced manufacturing.

Figures 8-6 and 8-7 illustrate some tips about setting targets. In Figure 8-6, instead of looking at percentages to set Cost Half targets, we ask you to first envision a target that would help strengthen the organization and then determine the values you must achieve to reach that target.

At some companies, teams chose "cut costs by half" as their organization-strengthening target. That is all well and good, since this is the Cost Half approach, but the team should also be prepared to explain what kind of outcome they envision when costs are cut by

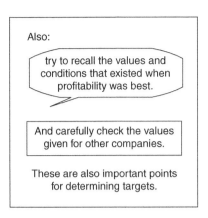

Also:

try to recall the values and
conditions that existed when
profitability was best.

And carefully check the values
given for other companies.

These are also important points
for determining targets.

Figure 8-7. More Tips About Setting Targets

about half. Having a clear vision of the outcome helps foster a positive attitude among Cost Half team members.

Determine "Acceptable Costs".   To achieve target costs, you have to
stop thinking about the target values and instead focus on what cost
level has been shown to be acceptable. When taking the Cost Half
approach, set three types of acceptable costs, the 1) acceptable item
cost, 2) acceptable process cost, and 3) acceptable product cost. The
way that item costs and process costs are viewed from the Cost Half
perspective was explained in Chapter 4. Acceptable costs are determined via a different method, as is illustrated in Figure 8-8. Here
there are several constituents of the acceptable product cost, including not only material costs, labor costs, and purchased goods costs
but also service and recycling costs

Figure 8-9 shows how acceptable item costs and acceptable
process costs are categorized and determined starting from the target cost level.

In the example in Figure 8-9, the acceptable item cost value is
88.05, while the acceptable process cost is 87.55 and the acceptable
product cost is 85. Since these values are in relation to the "100" index value of the total sales figure, if the total sales figure declines,
the acceptable costs will also decline accordingly. In this example,
the amount of cost reduction is slight, so the increase in operating
profit is only 4.5 points. Obviously, a more ambitious cost reduction
target would be needed in order to achieve a 10-point improvement
in the operating profit. At this point, the activity teams at several
companies decided to set their new acceptable cost by establishing a

This illustrates how the acceptable product cost can be determined. It may be necessary in some cases to include service & maintenance costs and recycling costs in the acceptable product cost.

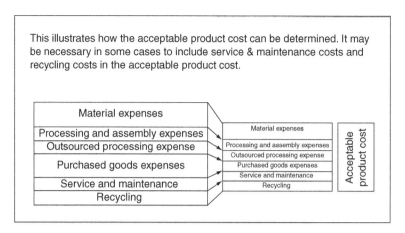

Figure 8-8. Constituents of the Acceptable Product Cost

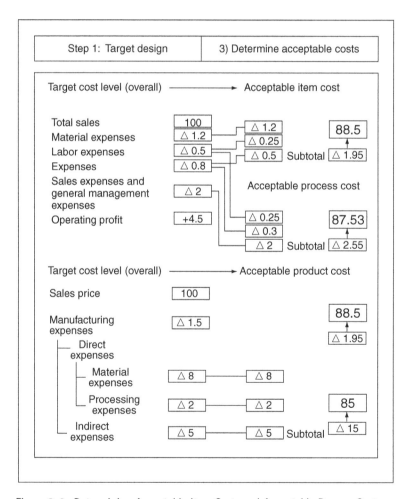

Figure 8-9. Determining Acceptable Item Costs and Acceptable Process Costs

50 percent (1/2) cost reduction as the goal of their activities. In such cases, the activity target is set separately from the acceptable target. Naturally, many activity teams try to set some kind of 50 percent reduction as a goal, since they are taking the "Cost Half" approach. And many activity teams actually have achieved their 50 percent cost reduction targets.

Now comes the deployment of the acceptable cost, which is the level where they must select the production processes, parts or units, and processes to be targeted for cost-cutting improvements. For item costs, this means analyzing the costs of parts and units; for process costs it means analyzing the costs of each core process; and for product costs it means analyzing the costs of parts, units, materials, and processing operations. In the example in Figure 8-9, the acceptable item cost is 88.05.

Allot Acceptable Costs.   To reduce item costs, first examine in some detail the costs by allocating more specific "acceptable item costs." Then set the cost targets. Item costs are allotted among different types of "items" as material expenses, part expenses, outsourced processing expenses, die expenses, and equipment expenses.

Next, you need an analysis to determine which specific item costs you should emphasize as improvement targets. Figure 8-10 shows the acceptable item cost value of 88.05 is made up of costs allotted to specific expense items such as material expenses, part expenses, and outside processing expenses. Before allotting these costs, you must study the current costs. After doing that, you can begin to set the direction for improvement activities. Cost analyses based on structure and expense-item categories can provide useful reference data. It is also important to consider the structure-related categories that will be emphasized.

Figure 8-11 shows an example of cost analysis of item costs. You could also use a Pareto diagram for this analysis. The essential thing is to find the points of emphasis among product structures and expense-item categories. Thus, the allotment of acceptable costs shown in Figure 8-10 is further deployed into structure and part categories in Figure 8-11. The categories to be used for this deployment of costs should be the categories that work best as activity targets. Usually, costs for emphasized parts are deployed as acceptable costs in part-related categories.

Similarly, process costs are allotted as acceptable process costs based on a consideration of the process costs to be emphasized. In

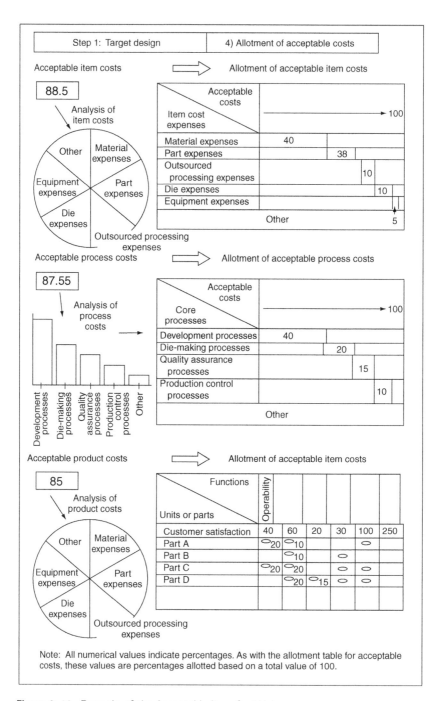

Figure 8-10. Example of the Acceptable Item Cost Value

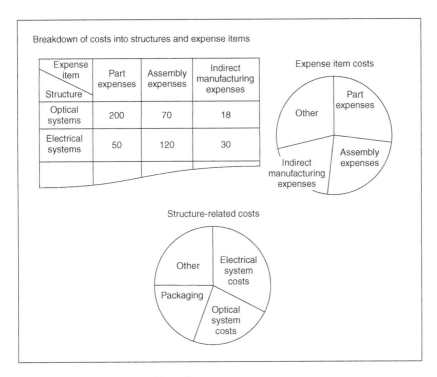

Figure 8-11. Cost Analysis of Item Costs

Figure 8-10, the allotment table places a lot of emphasis on development processes, which is typical among most companies. In the *work task process* category, processes that account for major cost generating sources should be determined separately for each type of business or industry. If it is the manufacturing industry, emphasis is placed on so-called *innovation processes* such as product development processes or technology development processes. These processes are critical not only as cost generating sources but also as generators of added value. Emphasis is also placed on operation processes that link sales operations with production and distribution operations. These are also known as production control processes or supply chain processes. In addition, quality assurance and equipment management processes may be emphasized.

To allot process costs as acceptable costs, break down the costs one level further than what is in Figure 8-10. In other words, determine targets for each step when tasks are performed as part of typical processes. A study of current costs is required in this case but, as is shown in Figure 8-12, the method used to study personnel requirements is a relatively easy method. Nevertheless, a variety of tasks are

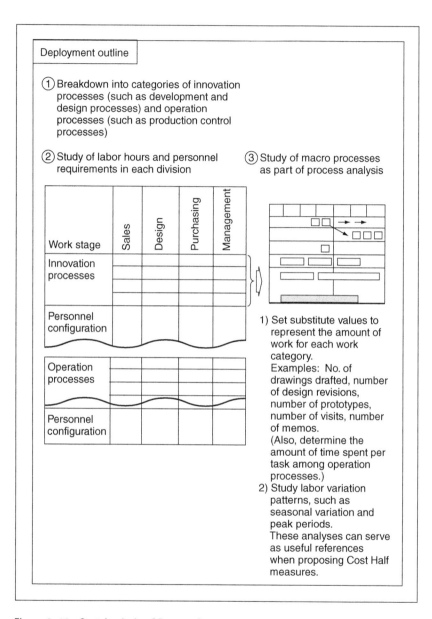

Figure 8-12. Cost Analysis of Process Costs

going on at the same time, and although you can obtain some information through interviews and by checking schedules, many tasks must be considered hypothetically. Since acceptable cost targets have already been set for process costs as a whole, these targets can now be further broken down into division-based or task function-based categories. This may involve taking some typical examples of product development processes and checking the work schedule of development personnel to determine the figure for labor hours.

Since acceptable costs have already been determined for processes in general (see Figure 8-10), to determine the acceptable process costs you simply allot these values to the individual processes. Even if allotment of specific values proves difficult, the acceptable costs are still a useful reference for evaluating the suitability of staffing levels.

Figure 8-13 brings together evaluations and requests from various divisions. This provides a new perspective for evaluating tasks, which serves as a reference for determining target values. In the case of work processes, you can organize the same chart around individual work processes. Of course, this chart is also useful for evaluating entire divisions.

Figure 8-14 shows process costs can be considered not only in the conventional way as costs of processes that occur in particular divisions, such as sales processes or production processes, but also as cross-divisional process costs that are linked to several divisions. Note how tasks that occur from early on in development and onward can all be thought of as a single process.

The process example shown in Figure 8-14 is a supply chain process. Conventionally, we would define separate processes such as a sales-production process, parts purchasing process, and product supply process. But in this example, there is only one process and it includes everything from users and consumers to production and materials purchasing. This not only provides a broader perspective on process change, it also promotes the development of truly innovative countermeasures against cost generating sources and locations. Figure 8-14 also lists several points to consider regarding process change.

Since the allotment of acceptable product costs is aimed at specific products, costs are allotted based on the parts and/or units that comprise the targeted products. As you saw in Figure 8-10, the functions that are involved with products are weighted in importance based on customer satisfaction scores, and then costs are allocated to parts. This method is especially effective when used for parts that have been revised to improve their marketability. The customer satisfaction score in this example is allotted from a total score of 250 points.

Step 2: Analysis of Cost Generating Sources and Locations

Clarifying cost generating sources and locations and then modifying both are a basic part of the Cost Half approach. It is not possible to

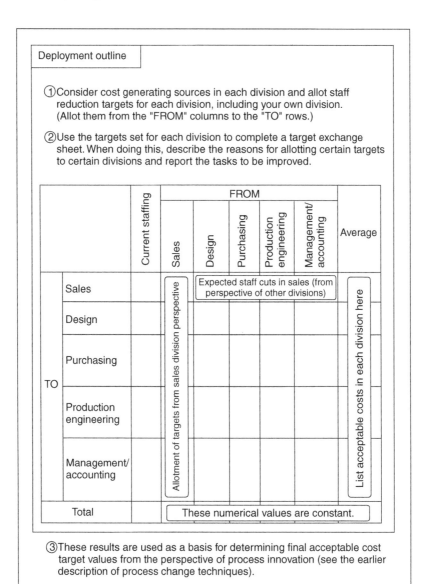

Figure 8-13. Allotment of Process Cost Target Values

make these changes in cost generating sources and their locations if we look at costs only in terms of totals for categories such as material costs and processing costs.

Where do costs occur? And why do they occur in those places? These are the sorts of questions you must ask in order to change costs. This type of cost analysis is not a result; it is merely a step to-

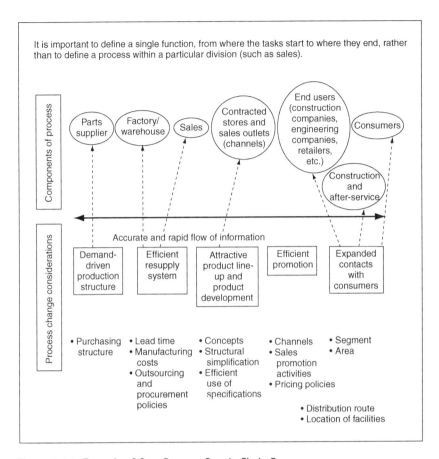

It is important to define a single function, from where the tasks start to where they end, rather than to define a process within a particular division (such as sales).

Figure 8-14. Example of Core Process: Supply Chain Process

ward reducing costs. At Step 1, we determined the cost targets and the acceptable costs that must be achieved. Using acceptable costs as a standard, what is the best way to manufacture things? How should processes be designed? These are questions to ask at Step 2.

Analysis of Cost Generating Locations. In Figure 8-15, we examine a part (package) as a cost generating location for a die cost (an item cost). The cost generating locations start with the cost incurred by the designer who designs the drawing of the part (package). Strictly speaking, the cost generating locations actually start from the product's conceptual design phase, but it is not until you reach the stage where part drawings are drafted that many design labor hours are devoted to the package as a part. The part drawings are created as part of the process design carried out by production engineers.

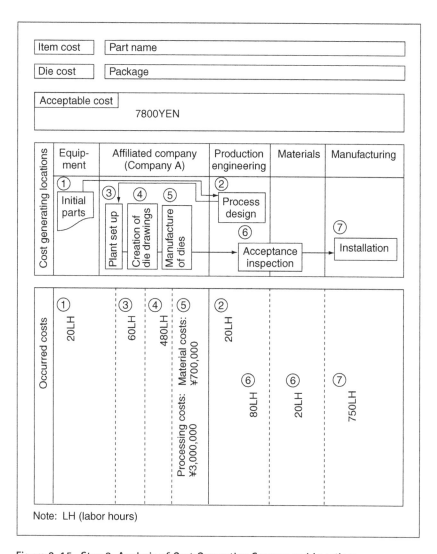

Figure 8-15. Step 2. Analysis of Cost Generating Sources and Locations:
① Analysis of Cost Generating Locations

This is one change in the location of cost generating sources. After the process design is completed, the die-making work at the next stage is farmed out to affiliated companies. This is another change in the location of cost generating sources.

When the die-making work is completed, the dies are shipped to the Production Engineering Division. There, the dies undergo an acceptance inspection. Though acceptance inspections are typically performed in cooperation with the Quality Assurance Division, at this company it was the Materials Division that helped with the acceptance inspections. Dies that pass these inspections are passed along to the Manufacturing Division, since that is the division responsible for making the boxes (packages).

Although the dies in the example passed the acceptance inspection the first time, it is not unusual for several inspections to be required before they pass. Thus, you have another instance of a new location for generating costs on one or perhaps several occasions. Since costs are incurred at each location and each occasion, such circumstances are a factor behind higher costs.

In each of the cost-related columns in Figure 8-15, there are figures for LH (labor hours), which means the number of working hours spent by employees. The cost of each working hour spent by the average employee can be expressed as a *charge* (labor rate), which is easily convertible into a monetary value. The manufacture of the metal dies incurs material costs and processing costs. The die cost is the sum of these costs.

However, sometimes you must also add other costs, such as the earnings of supplier companies and the associated distribution costs. Since the cost generating locations for item-cost things such as dies, jigs, tools, and other equipment are relatively large when evaluated on a per-item basis, it is best to deal with these cost locations from the design stage for the parts being used in production.

The amount entered in the *acceptable cost* part of the form in Figure 8-15 was as a reference value for the amounts allocated at Step 1. As such, it can help clarify differences with actually occurring costs.

Materials and parts are handled not only at the raw materials stage but also at various production processes such as machining and assembly processes. Although you can start considering process costs at the stage where drawings are created, it is more effective to consider the process costs for overall development/design processes rather than to study the process costs of individual parts.

The locations that generate process costs are the locations where work tasks are performed. The main set of core work processes where you might most readily find such locations are, in the case of manufacturing companies, the work processes related to development and design. Generally, cost generating locations at development/design processes start at the product planning stage. After that come the processes at the design, prototype testing, production setup, and initial production stages. In addition, there are various production management processes, quality assurance processes, and so on. All of these processes are target areas for cost reduction efforts. You can approach the cost generating locations as a flow that coincides with the flow of planning, design, and production. The analysis of these cost generating locations does not need to distinguish between in-house processes and processes at affiliated companies. However, in cases where some parts are jointly developed with affiliated companies, you must examine the joint processes in terms of the partners involved. In other words, there must not be any "rounding out" of numbers or other short cuts. The idea is to clarify all the details, and to avoid leaving any mysterious "black boxes."

Analysis of Cost Generating Sources.   Once you clarify the cost generating sources, you can begin looking into the difference between the acceptable costs and the actually occurring costs. You can expect to find quite a big gap between the two and closing it will require new ideas as to how to turn out products and restructure work processes in ways that achieve the acceptable costs.

The Cost Half approach toward brainstorming these ideas is to ask how you can change the cost generating sources and cost generating locations. The analysis illustrated in Figure 8-15 goes a long way toward clarifying cost generating locations but not cost generating sources. So you must also ask, "Why did those costs occur at those cost generating locations?"

Figure 8-16 shows you how to identify cost generating sources. This method is closely tied to the Cost Half techniques, so you should bear in mind how these techniques were defined in previous chapters.

As we discussed in Chapter 7, the three Cost Half techniques we use to that target item costs are, 1) changes in preconditions and limitations, 2) changes in structures, and 3) changes in logic. These three techniques help to identify and list the cost generating sources that you need to target for improvements. Figure 8-16 deals with item costs and lists the three Cost Half techniques along the vertical axis so you can develop (define) separately the cost generating sources (causes) under each technique.

The structural changes indicated in Figure 8-16 are directed at specific structural problems. What are these structural problems? Do you need to change product structures? In addition, when examining the reasons for having the current variety of parts, you need to ask how the combination of fixed and variable components are involved. All of this is part of cost generating causes.

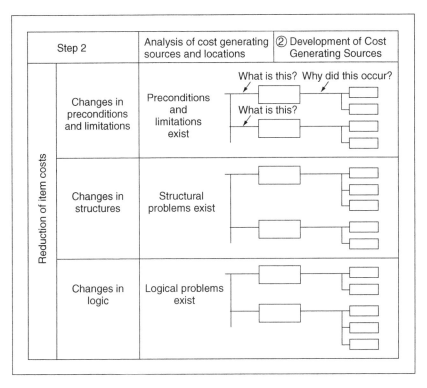

Figure 8-16. Development of Cost Generating Sources

You should focus the structural changes not only on product structures, but also on production sites, the distribution of production activities among those sites, as well as the structure of materials procurement. All of these areas must be investigated.

To take another example, let us see how you can make changes in preconditions and limitations. As Figure 8-16 shows, at the next level you repeatedly ask, "what is this?" In other words, you ask, "which preconditions and limitations exist in a way that generates costs?" When you have identified such a precondition or limitation, you then ask "why" it is a cost generator. Once you have reached this level in your analysis, it becomes possible to list quite a variety of cost generating sources. If cost generating sources do not become apparent even after asking these questions repeatedly, it is only because you are not pursuing the cost generating sources effectively. It is important to develop the ability to pursue cost generating sources.

Once you are experienced in identifying cost generating locations, it is only natural you will want to root out cost generating sources.

However, to effectively root out these sources, you must have a thorough understanding of the Cost Half techniques. Likewise, the Cost Half techniques are essential for reducing process costs as well. As was described in Figure 8-1, you apply PC (process changes) and AC (activity changes) when developing cost generating sources. It would be a good idea at this point to review the explanation of these techniques in Chapters 5 through 7, or refer back to Chapter 3 for a brief overview.

Figure 8-17 can help you understand how to analyze cost generating sources and their locations. The figure breaks costs down into established costs and occurring costs. Established costs are determined via design drawings and schedules. By contrast, occurring costs are

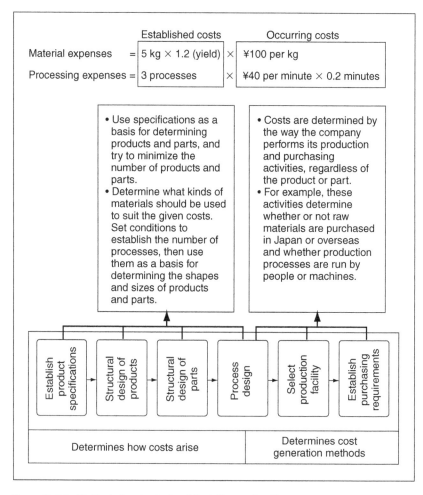

Figure 8-17. Methods for Analysis of Cost Generating Sources
and Cost Generating Locations

costs that occur at the factories of the manufacturing company and its suppliers. Even when the established costs are the same, their occurring costs tend to differ. In addition, a substantial reduction in established costs does not necessary mean a substantial reduction in occurring costs. That is why it is so important to study both types of costs when analyzing cost generating sources and locations. It is easy to focus only on the occurring costs, so be careful to avoid that pitfall.

Step 3: Apply the Five Cost Half Techniques to Propose Actions and Scenarios

At step 2, you saw how to analyze cost generating sources and their locations. In our example, separate teams performed the separate analyses for reducing item costs, process costs, and product costs. All of these analyses are performed to help design items, processes, and products whose costs are at or below the level of acceptable costs. When viewed from the perspective of acceptable costs, cost generating sources and cost generating locations are pursued as key points in the battle to close the cost gap between acceptable costs and current costs. By this stage, you should assume some view-points on Cost Half measures have already been proposed. However, don't assume that those measures will be adequate by themselves. That is because you have yet to fully apply the Cost Half techniques.

So at Step 3, Cost Half techniques are applied to help propose Cost Half measures as well as scenarios involving those measures. Note in Figure 8-18 the the first two numbered items, "① Target design" and "② Acceptable cost," are clearly established at Step 1, which deals specifically with designing targets. The third item, "③ Cost generating structures," is analyzed at Step 2 which focuses on cost generating sources and cost generating locations. Here at Step 3, we progress to the last three items: "⑤ View toward changing cost generating locations," "⑥ Changes," and "⑦ Cost Half scenarios."

The Cost Half Matrix—A Tool for Proposing Cost Half Scenarios. First comes the task of creating a Cost Half matrix that combines the cost generating sources and cost generating locations that were identified at Step 2. Of course, the goal is not simply to create a Cost Half matrix. The purpose of the Cost Half matrix is to help orient you in your efforts to change cost generating sources and their locations. It also helps you identify and remove bias and omissions from Cost Half measures. Finally, it is also a tool for estimating the effects of

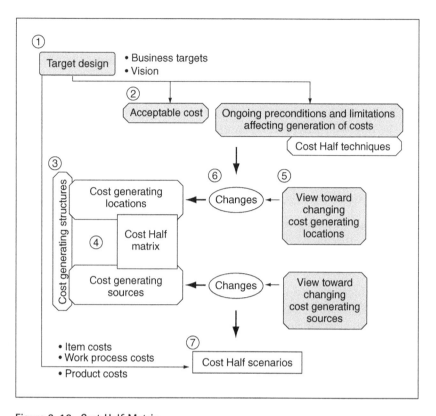

Figure 8-18. Cost Half Matrix

Cost Half measures. To help determine a proper orientation, you should be asking a few questions, such as:

- Can we be more effective by establishing connections between one cost generating location and another?
- Can we be more effective by establishing connections between one cost generating source and another?
- Can we come up with improvements that are more powerful by analyzing cost generating sources and locations collectively (at the unit or assembly level) rather than individually?
- Is it more effective to change cost generating locations than to change cost generating sources?
- Is it more effective to change cost generating sources than to change cost generating locations?

Indeed, there are many questions you can ask. Here's another one: since this is the Cost Half approach, should we seek to reduce by half the cost values of cost generating sources and cost generating locations? Figure 8-19 shows a simple example of a Cost Half matrix at

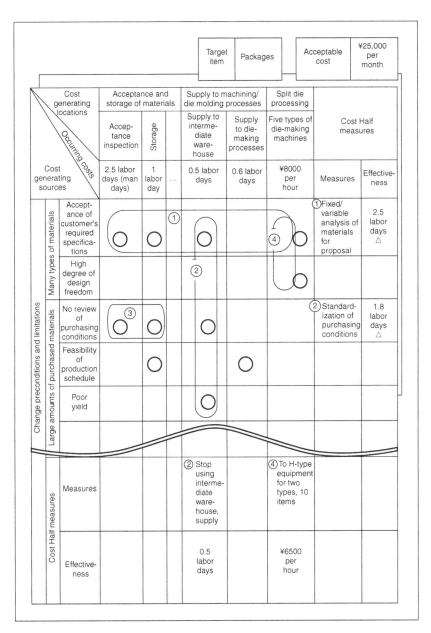

Figure 8-19. Using A Cost Half Matrix to Propose Cost Half Measures

work. For item costs, a unit for creating a Cost Half matrix should be determined by examining the importance in cost reduction among units, assembly, and parts. For process costs, we target the unit of product development process and production management process.

In this matrix, the cost generating sources are listed along the vertical axis, which represent some of the sources behind the company's preconditions and limitations. You can further develop the contents of this matrix using other techniques. All Cost Half techniques should be applied, and there is certainly no need to keep the matrix small enough to fit on one page.

The cost generating locations and occurring costs, which we have already discussed, are listed along the horizontal axis of the matrix. Circles appear in the matrix at the intersections of these vertical-axis and horizontal-axis items. In other words, each circle represents a point where a cost generating source meets a cost generating location. You can prioritize these intersection points by using different color circles to indicate levels of priority. At this point, use Cost Half techniques to plan Cost Half measures. Cost generating sources shown along the vertical axis in the matrix are analyzed by Cost Half techniques such as changing preconditions and limitations, and the structure (reduction of number of parts and processes). Therefore, we can develop Cost Half measures by asking:

- Can we reduce costs indicated at cost generating locations by changing preconditions and limitations?
- Can we reduce cost indicated at cost generating locations by changing the structure (reduction of number of parts and processes)?
- Can we reduce cost indicated at cost generating locations by changing the design logic?

For process costs, we can ask:

- Can we reduce costs indicated at cost generating locations by changing process change?
- Can we reduce cost indicated at cost generating locations by changing activity change?

Cost Half measures and estimates of effectiveness are listed along the right edge of the horizontal axis. Each Cost Half measure should be numbered and linked to corresponding cost generating sources or cost generating locations.

The measures listed along the vertical axis are chiefly aimed at changing cost generating locations, and estimates of the measures and their effectiveness appear at the bottom of the matrix. The measures shown in this part of the matrix are measures based on Cost Half techniques, such as were described in Chapters 5 through 7.

Figures 8-20 to 8-23 describe key points of Cost Half measures and provide a useful reference when selecting Cost Half measures from Cost Half matrix charts.

	Item costs	Material/part costs
Cost Half techniques	Cost generating sources	Points of emphasis in Cost Half measures
Change preconditions and limitations	• Surplus, excess, or unnecessary quality specification • Surplus, excess, or unnecessary function or quality specification	• Re-investigation of preconditions and limitations • Re-investigation of preconditions and limitations
Structural changes	• Variety of materials • Variety of parts • Too many parts due to "one part per function" policy	• Categorization of fixed components (including parts used in various products) and variable costs (parts that differ depending on their manufacturer). • One part per multiple functions • One part per multiple functions
Logic changes	• Existence of complicated parts • Existence of complicated assembly structure • Existence of large parts that are unnecessarily heavy	• Design for simplicity • Design for simplicity • Design for compactness

Figure 8-20. Key Points in Cost Half Measures

Step 4: Cost Half Measures and Results Management

Before implementing Cost Half measures, you must clarify the proposed measures as implementation themes. This involves not only clarifying the implementation themes themselves but also linking them to some kind of result. This is something that everyone involved should understand.

Another step that comes before implementation is creating Cost Half scenarios, which is illustrated in Figure 8-24.

Basically, Figure 8-24 summarizes the investigative process from the target design stage to the Cost Half implementation stage and helps you to see the overall flow of activities. Once you launch a Cost Half project, it generally takes at least three months to reach this stage. This figure provides you an opportunity to reaffirm the purpose

		Item costs	Material/part costs
Cost Half techniques	Cost generating sources	Points of emphasis in Cost Half measures	
Change preconditions and limitations	• Variation in purchase unit prices • Complexity of purchasing structure • Establishment of too many production processes (especially inspection processes)	• Review of unit prices, elimination of preconditions • Intensification and simplification of structure of purchased goods and suppliers • Investigation of preconditions and limitations	
Structural changes	• Too many process routes • Too many types of production processes • Too many production processes • Too many types of machines and dies • Too many machines and dies • Too many production sites	• Fixed/variable analysis of production process routes and types • Redesign multi-function production processes and multi-process stages • Fixed/variable analysis of machines and dies • Design more machine and die functions into each machine unit, design machine units for multiple processes • Intensify production sites	
Logic changes	• Existence of complicated production processes	• Design simpler processes	

Figure 8-21. Key Points in Cost Half Measures

and goals of Cost Half activities and plans for implementing Cost Half measures. It is also an opportunity to add any new ideas.

First, briefly review the basic concepts of Cost Half activities. Next, envision the kind of business operations to be realized by implementing Cost Half measures. Estimate the overall target cost based on the target profitability ratio. After that, start identifying cost generating locations and cost generating sources. Use a Cost Half matrix as an aid in devising Cost Half measures.

After putting together the Cost Half measures, start defining the item specifications (for products, parts, production processes, dies, etc.) to be achieved as well as the process specifications (development work

	Item costs	Material/part costs
Cost Half techniques	Cost generating sources	Points of emphasis in Cost Half measures
Change preconditions and limitations	• Series type assignments of work process steps and responsibilities in divisions • No management of project tasks and division's tasks • Weak control points	• Introduce more parallel processing • Employment of project managers • Review of preconditions and limitations
PC (process changes)	• Overloaded at downstream processes, too many follow-up tasks • Too much reworking and re-checking	• Source rationalization • Implementation of them-based management
AC (activity changes)	• Too many manual operations • Too many memos and reports • Elimination of skills gap between veterans and newer employees	• Adoption of CAD tools, etc. • Adoption of communication tools, etc. • Co-location • Increased use of knowledge management tools

Figure 8-22. Key Points in Cost Half Measures

processes, supply chain and quality control processes, etc.). It is imperative that the things you want to achieve are defined clearly so everyone
can understand them. It is also important to clarify the implementation
system and results management schedule behind each scenario. It bears
repeating that, when proposing scenarios, your focus should be on envisioning the kind of product, process, and/or production structure that
you wish to establish by implementing Cost Half measures.

Item ⑦ in Figure 8-24 is "Measures to reduce item costs and implemented item specifications." For this, you need to elucidate factors such
as the specifications for products or production processes, the structure
of products or production processes, and the structure of purchasing.
This information comes together as something like a catalog, which
you might call a hypothetical catalog at this point. You also need to
put together similar information for the work processes corresponding

	Item costs	Material/part costs

Cost Half techniques	Cost generating sources	Points of emphasis in Cost Half measures
Change preconditions and limitations	• Lead time for delivery to market • Greater amounts of diverted inventory • Higher transportation costs • Imbalanced or excessive functions among distributor contractors and sales offices • Distribution quality (quality, dating control, etc.)	• Establish different lead times based on sales policies • Review logic of delivery and shipment timing • Integrate and intensify transport trips • Change logic of unit pricing • Integrate prior shipments and deliveries • Optimize delivery vehicle usage, use larger vehicles • Employ consignment companies • Change preconditions
PC (process changes)	• Inadequate integration of manufacturing and sales • Inadequate management and sharing of source information • Lengthening of process lead time due to series type processes	• Greater emphasis on process timing to improve internal conflicts • Greater linearity • Source management of information production, distribution, and revision • Expansion of functions among relevant divisions and affiliated companies to make progress toward seamless processes
AC (activity changes)	• Too many manual operations • Too many adjustments • Too much standby time	• Use GPC tools, etc. • Use communication tools • More multi-function skills

Figure 8-23. Key Points in Cost Half Measures

to item ⑧ and the Cost Half implementation targets corresponding to item ⑨ in Figure 8-24. The kinds of operations envisioned at this stage will be targeted by other Cost Half activities later on.

Creating an Implementation Schedule.   At this point, you create an overall schedule for the implementation stage. There must be some kind of deadline (e.g., which quarter of which business year) for reaching the target cost levels. This means there must also be a sched-

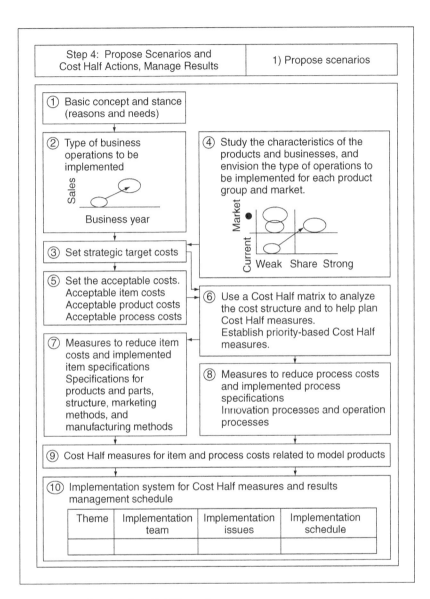

Figure 8-24. Creating Cost Half Scenarios

ule stating which Cost Half activities you need to complete and by when (and for which products). Before entering Cost Half activities onto this schedule, prioritize them. For example, you might ask when a certain target item for cost reduction needs to be addressed by Cost Half activities for current products within the product group (and products for the next two or three years), and then set the implementation schedule accordingly.

The implementation schedule should include one "milestone" of progress about every six months and events such as presentations of reports to top managers. The activities may need some fine-tuning along the way or may even need to be reoriented. You should also work into the schedule checkpoints to consider such options.

Establishment of Organization to Promote Implementation. The members of the implementation teams must be of a high enough caliber to work at the level of proposed Cost Half scenarios and other key concepts. Here, many companies face problems in trying to determine who they can use as full-time implementation team members. It is always best to have at least some implementation team members serve as full-time members, but not all companies have enough human resources available to do that.

At each stage, from proposing scenarios to planning concepts and implementing activities, there are more and more things that you will need to study or provide which will increase the number of people you will need for the Cost Half activities. It is always best to have as many full-time implementation team members as possible. However, there is no need for all implementation team members to be full-time members. The important thing is establish a group of core members for the proposal of ideas, as a group separate from those who create the scenarios, and then the core members can later enlist the aid of other members.

The themes used for Cost Half implementation projects are likely to be issues that exist in the members' daily product development work, or other work in various divisions. Consequently, the members who have proposed scenarios take these activity theme proposals to their respective divisions, and it is within the various divisions that people can ponder how to approach the issue from the perspective of their daily work.

Cost Half Measures. Figure 8-25 illustrates the steps used to implement Cost Half measures. These steps start with management of hypotheses, including the clarification of relevant issues, and include planning implementation schedules and carrying out implementation.

Since measures are only hypothetical before they are implemented, you should consider ways to verify the measures. Next comes planning the promotion schedule and then comes implementation itself. You need to manage the results at each of these steps.

The project manager and ad-hoc meetings both have important roles to play in results management. The key to success is to implement according to the master plan, verify results, and then promptly continue with the next implementation item.

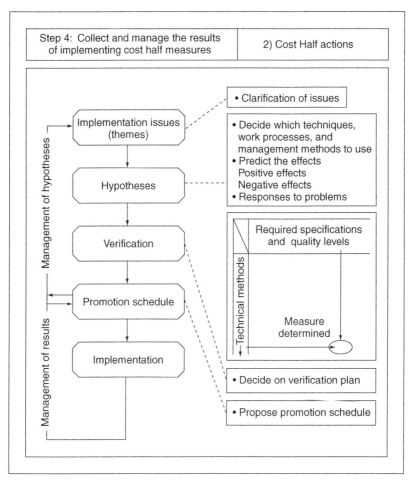

| Step 4: Collect and manage the results of implementing cost half measures | 2) Cost Half actions |

Figure 8-25. Steps to Implement Cost Half Measures

As indicated in Figure 8-26, there are three types of results to be managed: 1) results of measures, 2) results of promotion, and 3) results relative to targets. Check often to make sure that items you targeted with your implementation measures are being implemented on schedule, and that you are achieving expected results.

Progress management means keeping implementation on schedule. You cannot expect much in terms of results if you do not implement measures as planned. Accordingly, progress managers must work to clear away obstacles and keep implementation progressing smoothly.

Results relative to targets means determining whether or not the implementation has achieved the Cost Half targets. These targets are defined as *overall cost levels* and *product-specific cost levels*. You should evaluate both types of targets.

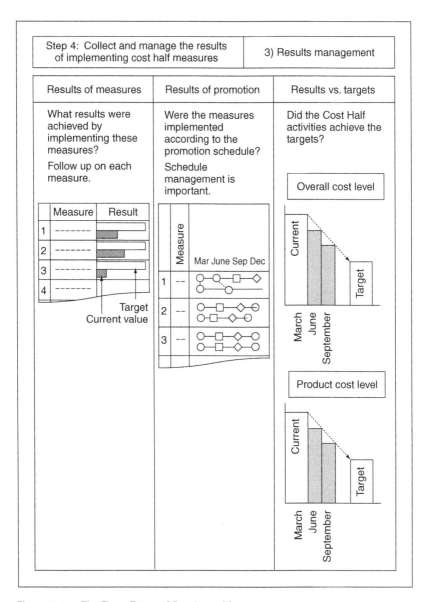

Figure 8-26. The Three Types of Results to Manage

Step 5: Build and Operate a Cost Half Cost Management System

One might reasonably ask why there is a need for a Cost Half cost management system. Typically, after you have completed the product development, a series of cost reduction projects are implemented to resolve various cost-related issues. However, performing one such project after another is wasteful and represents a loss of opportunity. Like a quality management system, a Cost Half cost management system is essential. But if that is the case, then why don't more companies build and operate such systems?

One reason is that managers do not understand costs among design processes and therefore do not know how to manage them. They do not know how to create a Cost Management Division, how to allocate target costs (as improvement targets) to various other divisions, or how to promote and manage the results.

Another reason is that managers do not track costs well enough. They may work hard to set cost targets, but they do not know how to follow up on them. Without effective follow-up, there really is no management of costs.

A Cost Half cost management system has three phases: 1) strategic phase, 2) development/design phase, and, 3) production/supply phase. Figure 8-27 illustrates the activities that take place during these three phases. The overall goal is to realize the desired outcome that was envisioned at the start.

At the strategic phase, you set cost targets based on cost strategies and cost development for the mid-term future (three to five years). The idea is to build the cost structures that are needed to build a stronger, more competitive organization. In addition, the overall goal is to achieve the overall target cost level. To do that, you need to set various cost levels for major products, and this cost-setting activity must be based on market studies to determine competitive sales prices. In this situation, early development of certain key parts or units for new products may be needed inasmuch as the new products may require new production processes and work processes. This is part of "cost development."

It is at the development/design phase where previous experience in Cost Half projects can prove quite useful for you. Cost design is implemented starting from the point where you first seek to define target costs, acceptable costs and how they are allocated, as well as cost generating sources and their locations. Next, you begin to propose Cost Half measures and scenarios of desired outcomes. This is the phase where costs are determined.

At the production/supply phase, you continue to implement improvements while tracking variation in costs at production and supply processes. Naturally, you must do whatever you can to keep costs below the target levels that were set back at the cost design phase. To do that, you must track the costs. This also requires the ability to

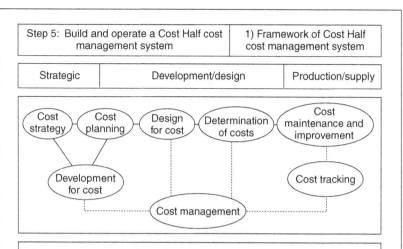

Step 5: Build and operate a Cost Half cost management system | 1) Framework of Cost Half cost management system

| Strategic | Development/design | Production/supply |

Cost strategy — Cost planning — Design for cost — Determination of costs — Cost maintenance and improvement

Development for cost

Cost tracking

Cost management

Cost management can be defined as setting profitability levels as targets and performing activities starting from the early product planning stages to ensure that each new product meets its target cost.

For cost managers, applying managerial techniques to find solutions that meet the company's particular circumstances is even more important than applying cost-cutting methods.

Although the practice of cost management starting from the early product developing stages in not new, it has been beset with many problems due to increasingly short development lead times, which have not left enough time to fully investigate cost issues and devise effective measures, so it is becoming more and more likely that conventional cost management efforts will fail to achieve their goals.

As a result, cost management methods must be increasingly focused on intermediary strategic levels, such as the cost strategy and cost development phases illustrated above.

Figure 8-27. The Activities that Occur During the Three Phases of the Cost Half Management System

accurately gather and store cost data, such as materials purchasing data and production cost data. It is surprising how many companies do not yet have this ability. I would encourage such companies to build a Cost Half cost management system.

Figure 8-28 draws associations between items implemented under the Cost Half program and the Cost Half cost management system that was just described.

This concludes our step-by-step description of the five Cost Half activities necessary for the implementation of a Cost Half project. In our concluding Chapter we will provide useful Cost Half benchmarks to help you determine where you should begin your Cost Half activities.

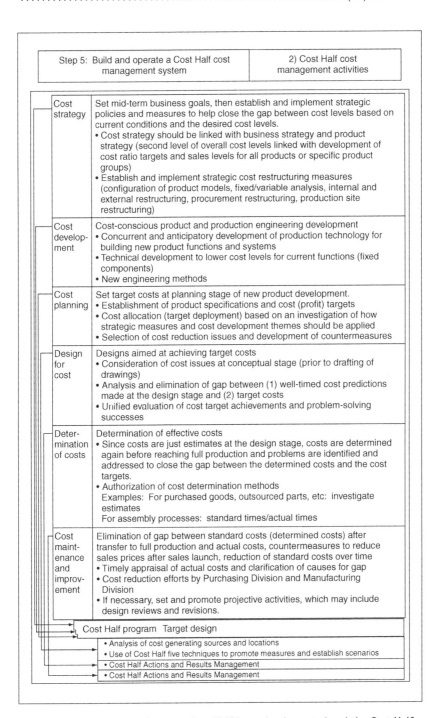

Step 5: Build and operate a Cost Half cost management system	2) Cost Half cost management activities

Cost strategy	Set mid-term business goals, then establish and implement strategic policies and measures to help close the gap between cost levels based on current conditions and the desired cost levels. • Cost strategy should be linked with business strategy and product strategy (second level of overall cost levels linked with development of cost ratio targets and sales levels for all products or specific product groups) • Establish and implement strategic cost restructuring measures (configuration of product models, fixed/variable analysis, internal and external restructuring, procurement restructuring, production site restructuring)
Cost development	Cost-conscious product and production engineering development • Concurrent and anticipatory development of production technology for building new product functions and systems • Technical development to lower cost levels for current functions (fixed components) • New engineering methods
Cost planning	Set target costs at planning stage of new product development. • Establishment of product specifications and cost (profit) targets • Cost allocation (target deployment) based on an investigation of how strategic measures and cost development themes should be applied • Selection of cost reduction issues and development of countermeasures
Design for cost	Designs aimed at achieving target costs • Consideration of cost issues at conceptual stage (prior to drafting of drawings) • Analysis and elimination of gap between (1) well-timed cost predictions made at the design stage and (2) target costs • Unified evaluation of cost target achievements and problem-solving successes
Determination of costs	Determination of effective costs • Since costs are just estimates at the design stage, costs are determined again before reaching full production and problems are identified and addressed to close the gap between the determined costs and the cost targets. • Authorization of cost determination methods Examples: For purchased goods, outsourced parts, etc: investigate estimates For assembly processes: standard times/actual times
Cost maintenance and improvement	Elimination of gap between standard costs (determined costs) after transfer to full production and actual costs, countermeasures to reduce sales prices after sales launch, reduction of standard costs over time • Timely appraisal of actual costs and clarification of causes for gap • Cost reduction efforts by Purchasing Division and Manufacturing Division • If necessary, set and promote projective activities, which may include design reviews and revisions.

Cost Half program   Target design

- Analysis of cost generating sources and locations
- Use of Cost Half five techniques to promote measures and establish scenarios
- Cost Half Actions and Results Management
- Cost Half Actions and Results Management

Figure 8-28. Associations Between Cost Half Items Implemented and the Cost Half Cost Management System

9

Cost Half Benchmarks

Many companies are working harder than ever to boost product competitiveness and improve profitability. There are various background factors that make such efforts necessary, but they differ from company to company. However, all of them recognize that the market environment is so harsh that companies cannot survive unless they significantly reduce their cost levels.

The Cost Half approach has been well received at many companies, and many more plan to introduce it. Some companies have already chalked up major successes with this approach, while others are still in the midst of their Cost Half activities or are about to begin them.

One thing you must decide when introducing the Cost Half approach at your company is the scope of its implementation. Ultimately, when benchmarking various industries that have implemented Cost Half activities, you will find that it is best to implement Cost Half companywide. To begin with, though, a company should only apply the Cost Half approach to a principal aspect of its operations and, after achieving successful results, gradually extend the implementation throughout the company. In some cases, Cost Half implementation has been successfully implemented one factory at a time.

This chapter introduces four case studies that provide a wealth of reference material related to Cost Half promotion systems, targets, results, and follow-ups to Cost Half activities. It provides a few brief accounts from companies that have implemented Cost Half, which should prove useful to those seeking to further strengthen their Cost Half activities.

GAINING OUTSTANDING COMPETITIVENESS IN ATTRACTING ORDERS

Company A began a Cost Half program by centering cost-cutting activities on their development and design departments. Actually, they had already tried several times to implement cost-cutting activities to reduce costs for various specific products, and were anxious this time to succeed with the Cost Half approach.

The chief of the design division was appointed as the promotional leader. The overall goal was to lower cost levels to the point where they could reduce the sales prices of their major products by 30 percent. So far, they had reached a dead end in their efforts to achieve this goal, for reasons such as the following.

1. Activities that are centered on designers have only a limited range of cost reduction targets. In other words, the individuals in this case worked from drawings to devise ways to reduce costs mainly in materials, processing, and assembly labor, but were unable to address managerial and other indirect costs, which account for about 40 percent of total costs.
2. There was inadequate cooperation among the production engineering, materials and procurement, and manufacturing divisions, and people tended to leave too many decisions up to the design division.
3. Progress was slowed by the unexpectedly long time required to coordinate design spec revisions with the marketing division and sales division.
4. Proposals made by designers were too modest and failed to go "outside the box" of previous proposals.

In sum, the main problem in this case was that the company expected to somehow make substantial cost reductions without having to go beyond its traditional ways of thinking and working.

Cost Reduction Activities that Reach the Very Core of the Company

After meeting with managers at Company A, we came up with the schedule of Cost Half activities shown in Figure 9-1. We must emphasize that *these were not product cost reduction activities centered*

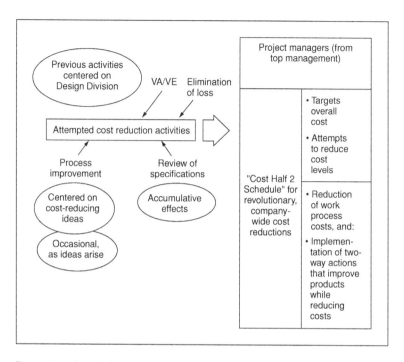

Figure 9-1. Revolutionary, Company-wide Cost Reductions

on design, but rather were companywide activities to reduce costs throughout the organization.

When cost reduction activities reach into the very core of the company, they can reduce cost levels for fixed expenses regardless of the design drawings. They are especially effective in reducing costs when the design drawings chiefly consist of variable expenses. Accordingly, the activities must be based not only on reforming product design and manufacturing but also individuals' daily work processes.

Activities Led by Project Managers and Top Management

Figure 9-2 shows that the main impetus for Cost Half activities comes from project management via the company's top managers, down through the various divisional and interdivisional leaders who have been appointed according to the project theme. In this case, there are effectively two kinds of themes to promote: 1) themes centered in a particular division and 2) themes promoted jointly by several divisions.

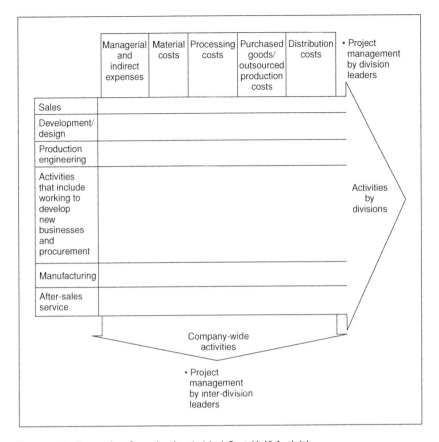

Figure 9-2. Promotion Organization behind Cost Half Activities

An appointed division manager (such as the head of the design division) typically manages themes of the former type. Themes of the latter type—joint projects that may involve designers, production engineers, and manufacturing staff—are usually managed by the chief of the production engineering division. Overall, the company's top managers (such as directors and division managers) carry out project management. Having such a combination of themes and managers in the promotion organization helps to extend Cost Half activities companywide and can make a big difference in the results achieved.

By switching from activities led by the design department head to a companywide set of activities led by top managers, Company A was able to go well beyond the scope of its previous cost reduction activities.

ACTIVITIES THAT INCLUDE WORKING TO DEVELOP NEW BUSINESSES

The concrete results of Cost Half projects depend on success at reducing fixed costs such as managerial and indirect costs, so it is important to find and eliminate unnecessary staffing. In other words, the idea is to rebuild the organization so that fewer and more able people run its existing businesses. Meanwhile, the company will free up resources needed to develop new businesses or products. Thus, implementation of Cost Half activities are effective enough to reduce costs on the one hand while promoting new business development on the other hand.

When Efforts to Develop New Businesses Are Added to Cost Half Activities

Company B initially planned cost reduction activities to focus on material costs in response to market needs. However, they recognized that reducing fixed costs is essential if they were to lower cost levels. Since the fixed costs were mainly personnel costs, they also recognized that they could not significantly reduce such costs by a simple set of activities.

Wherever there are people, there are costs, and costs and labor are the two essential components for creating or adding value. After meeting with managers at Company B, we established a Cost Half project to generate new business. This project's outcomes included a massive increase in companywide added value.

Management of Multiple Projects

During a Cost Half project, once you have established the scenario, it is time to appoint the people who will concurrently be in charge of promoting specific activity themes. You can expect some of these activity themes to go smoothly, while others are likely to encounter hindrances.

As far as Company B was concerned, the major theme was to keep the various activity themes on track in order to reach their targets despite whatever problems might arise. To accomplish that, they adopted some *multiproject management methods*. To begin with, they clarified the configuration of themes by establishing hierarchical and multilevel associations among them, which made it much easier to comprehend. In addition, they selected promotional topics for each theme and established a promotion schedule. The promotion leaders made it their objective to devise various ways to apply:

1. Project management functions.
2. Promotion topic-setting functions.
3. Technical information gathering and development abilities.
4. Guidance functions to stay on track toward achieving the envisioned results.

They also set up a theme progress monitoring program that monitored both quality and on-schedule timing, and could be accessed via the company's computer network. Figure 9-3 proves that the Cost Half strategy of training younger staff members to vigorously promote Cost Half projects is a very effective strategy indeed.

Figure 9-4 illustrates how such a program for developing new businesses draws its strength from capacity freed from every stage, from product planning to product development and sales.

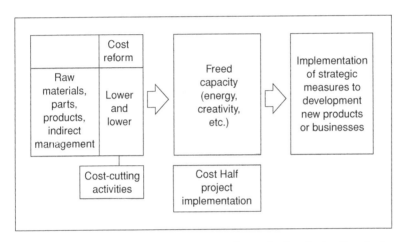

Figure 9-3. How Cost Reform Generates New Energy for Developing New Businesses

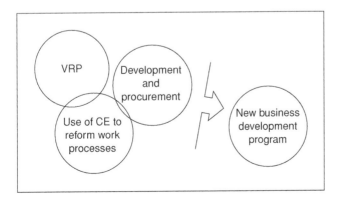

Figure 9-4. Cost Half's Basic Approach

RAISING THE PROFIT-SALES RATE

At Company C, a cosmetics company, employees were very worried because their company's sales figures were looking dreary compared to the competition. The world's best-run companies generally enjoy a profit-sales rate of about 7 or 8 percent. By contrast, Company C's rate was 1.5 to 2 percent.

Although Company C had some hit products, its cost levels were so high that it became difficult to turn much of a profit. Consequently, Company C launched a Cost Half project aimed at raising the profit-sales rate to at least 5 percent.

Cost Half Implementation for Specific Product Groups

One key factor for Company C was the configuration of its Cost Half promotion. The company had five domestic factories and six overseas factories, and each factory turned out several product groups. In other words, product groups were allocated among the factories as needed, based on distribution and sales conditions. Conversely, this meant that each product group was being manufactured at two or three different factories.

For that reason, it appeared it would be more effective to form Cost Half project teams based on product groups rather than the usual practice of forming teams based on individual factories. Consequently, their Cost Half project was initiated with three teams, one each for Product Group A, Product Group B, and Product Group C. Of course, each team understood that they were responsible for certain production processes at every factory that handled their product group.

After elucidating the characteristics of the product group they were responsible for, each team set its own specific goal. They framed these goals in terms of cost levels related to the profit-sales rate (the reduction of which was the overall goal of the project), such as the "acceptable item cost level," "acceptable process cost level," and "core product cost level."

Integration of Production Processes

The primary goals of Company C's Cost Half efforts were to integrate production processes and make a big reduction in indirect cost levels. They wanted to achieve the former by reducing the number of production lines by about two-thirds. Thus they concentrated on finding inexpensive ways to integrate production processes. For example, in a factory where there are 18 production processes, they decided to use processes 1 to 13 for all product types while reserving processes 14 to 18 for variable production of different product types. To do this, they had to review their distribution processes, where they discovered many cost generating sources and launched several Cost Half activity measures to eliminate them. Naturally, distribution processes change when production processes are integrated or when you otherwise modify production sites. As Company C looked ever deeper into their production system, they also found that the manner in which they had allocated production processes was based on preconceptions and preconditions rather than being market needs or business requirements.

4:6 Type Business Processes

As described earlier, if you plot a curve representing the trend of labor hour data from business processes from start to finish, about 40 percent of the labor hours appears on the first half of the curve and the other 60 percent on the second half. Such a configuration of business processes is called *4:6 type business processes*. In Company C's case, labor hours distributed among product planning and development processes also make a 4:6 type trend curve. In other words, most of the labor hours accrue at later processes. Not only that, but most of those downstream labor hours were for backtracking type work such as rework, duplicated work, or corrective work. They found that the PC (process changes) technique was particularly effective and were able to reduce costs based on labor hours by a remarkable 65 percent. This meant they were able to reassign some staff to work on new materials development and boost their new product development efforts by 20 percent. The ratio of hit products also rose 5 percent.

The company's previous abundance of production management processes contained a number of cost generating sources and locations. In particular, managers had been passing a lot of information among divisions, there had been many modifications and corrections, and several past attempts at restructuring had yielded weak results in terms of making real improvements or reforms.

A Systematic Approach Based on Product Groups
Proved Advantageous

At Company C, Cost Half implementation raised the sales-profit rate to within 5 percent of the target. Two years later, the sales-profit rate stood at 4.3 percent. Reaching 5 percent would take some time, as it involved a number of staff reassignments. Unlike the weak attempts at improvement in the past, this organizationwide approach based on product groups proved advantageous and was a powerful approach for boosting the sales-profit rate.

PULLING AHEAD OF THE COMPETITION IN DEVELOPING COST-COMPETITIVE NEW PRODUCTS

Company D, which is in an industry with only modest future growth expectations, introduced Cost Half activities aimed at improving both efficiency and enthusiasm. Some of these enthusiasm-related activities sought to improve distribution, some to improve production processes, and others to reform development processes. However, the sum total of these improvements was not enough to boost their business performance figures to the intended levels.

To begin, they interviewed all managers who ranked as division heads or above and sought their input regarding how best to introduce Cost Half activities. What people hope to gain from Cost Half implementation varies depending on their type of business, and in this case they found the most common expectation was to quickly raise the company's profitability. In this context "quickly" meant from six months to a year.

They were also anxious to speed up their new product development program. At the same time, they needed to reduce their cost levels substantially. Naturally, this meant having to reduce development lead time. Company D managers also voiced concern about eliminating production problems, which often were experienced immediately after entering full production.

Yet another problem faced by Company D was their wide array of subsidiary companies, which had spawned in great number before anyone had quite realized it. Many of these subsidiary companies were manufacturers; some were sales firms. The number of subsidiaries had increased in connection with Company D's own growth, and with this expansion came higher and higher management expenses and indirect expenses. Company D's overall cost structure was continually worsening.

Company D launched their Cost Half activities with a view toward resolving these types of problems. Before starting, however, they trained Cost Half team members for a month. (The type of training described earlier in this book as the training of "greedy members.") Naturally, members selected from various company divisions and trained in this program later played central roles in the Cost Half activities. As Figure 9-5 shows, Company D established a plan for approximately two years' worth of Cost Half activities.

During the first year, these activities were centered on three themes: 1) cutting item costs by half, 2) cutting process costs by half, and, 3) reforming new product development processes. During the second year, they sought to achieve higher goals in similar themes and also started restructuring certain business operations. These restructuring efforts included redesigning processes related to "buying, making, and developing," envisioning desired business conditions, strengthening core functions, and integrating functions to eliminate those that were unnecessary or redundant.

The Cost Half teams in charge of cutting item costs by half focused their activities on materials, purchased goods, dies, and consumables. They developed Cost Half measures centered on various restructuring techniques. As a result, they were able to achieve their target costs by about 30 percent after just six months of activities.

The Cost Half teams in charge of cutting process costs focused on cost generating sources and cost generating locations that can be found in many development and design processes. They formed a separate team to take on the task of reforming product development

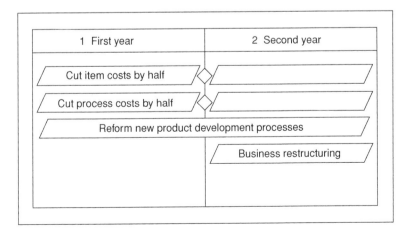

Figure 9-5. Company D's Cost Half Activities

processes, so they were able to clarify common elements early on, which helped spur the progress of their activities.

These commonly found cost generating sources and locations were addressed by activities focused on prototypes and testing, outsourced design work, production setup, manufacture of dies, equipment, and tools. In addition to development and design processes, their process cost reduction efforts dealt with process costs related to receiving customer orders, manufacturing, the supply chain, and sales. Although you usually address sales processes separately from production management costs, in Company D's case they thought it was important to link the two in support of their business restructuring efforts.

One year after launching their Cost Half activities, Company D's item cost reduction teams and process cost reductions teams had both begun to achieve solid results. The new product development process cost reduction team had managed to thoroughly improve the source management aspect of new product development, and they were becoming quite effective in shortening lead time.

THE COST HALF PROGRAM IS NOT MEANT
FOR HALFWAY MEASURES

As we mentioned at the beginning of the chapter, one of the first things you will have to do when introducing a Cost Half program at your company is to determine the scope of its implementation. We suggested that you begin by applying the Cost Half approach to a principal part of the company. Then, as you gain success, gradually implement the Cost Half approach to other parts of the company until, ultimately, you are applying it companywide. The Cost Half program will not be effective if pursued with halfhearted measures, or deployed as an ad hoc approach to cost cutting, or if used for making small, gradual improvements and piecemeal cost reductions, or as a temporary program of activities! The Cost Half approach is a set of systematic cost reduction methods and techniques that are geared toward achieving two types of cost competitiveness at the same time: the ability to improve the bottom line and the ability to maintain strongly competitive product costs. Using the Cost Half approach for any other reason will be ineffectual.

Postscript

The activity of reducing costs calls for a variety of skills and knowledge. Product development skills are needed, of course, as is knowledge about production process design and production management. Accordingly, after completing implementation of Cost Half activities, many team members find they have become better-skilled and more knowledgeable people. Little wonder, then, that the Cost Half approach to cost-cutting activities has often drawn the participation of company employees who had always shied away from getting involved.

Let us suppose that a company's Cost Management Division has set a cost reduction target. The next step is to get in touch with relevant personnel in other divisions. For instance, design staff may be enlisted to take part in activities aimed at cutting costs at the design stage. Unless they are shown a new way, the design staff will use the same old methods and will not learn new skills. Consequently, success will be limited. The same holds true in other company divisions as well. Soon, the Cost Management Division people who started the cost-cutting project get frustrated, since everyone is following the same old procedures and getting nowhere, and it becomes a vicious circle.

The Cost Half program starts by getting companies to question seriously the value of their conventional approach to cost-cutting activities. Companies learn to reorient their cost reduction activities by starting out not only with some business targets but also with a vision of how far they wish to go in boosting the competitiveness of their products. Naturally, Cost Half teams must enlist members who are able to deal with the issues at hand. But it is also important to provide training that bolsters the skills and knowledge of team members.

The attitude of those involved in Cost Half activities should not be one of overblown frugality. Rather, the idea is to cleverly devise new work processes and products that achieve an acceptable level of cost reduction (referred to in this book as the "acceptable cost"). In other words, you should understand the activity of cost cutting as a creative activity.

The quickest and easiest way to understand the Cost Half program is to try it out. Those who do not wish to dive into a full-fledged Cost Half program may choose instead to wade into it by implementing Cost Half activities only for a certain sample product or part, as was mentioned in this book's description of the "greedy members" training course. But in the end, for the Cost Half program to be fully effective, it must be fully engaged throughout the company.

I am confident that this book has much to offer to today's companies. Readers are invited to send me their questions or comments at the following email address: *suzue@consultainment.com*

Index

For Product Safety Concerns and Information please contact
our EU representative GPSR@taylorandfrancis.com Taylor & Francis
Verlag GmbH, Kaufingerstraße 24, 80331 München, Germany

T - #0025 - 230425 - C0 - 229/152/9 [11] - CB - 9781563272493 - Gloss Lamination